Give 'em JESUS!

The Only Soul Winner's Handbook You Will Ever Need

Complete With Explanations, Illustrations, Scripts and Applications for Overcoming Objections, False Doctrine and Cults

fred hege

T0015764

Give 'em Jesus ©2023 property of Just Give 'em Jesus.

All rights are the property of Just Give 'em Jesus, a 501(c) (3) Corporation whose mission statement is: To equip the Body of Christ around the world to be practical, passionate soul winners.

All rights reserved. No part of this book may be reproduced or transmitted in any form or by any means, electronic or mechanical, including photocopying, recording or by any information storage and retrieval system, without permission in writing from the copyright owner's board.

Published by Carpenter's Son Publishing, Franklin, Tennessee

All Scriptures in this book, unless otherwise noted, are quoted from The Holy Bible, ESV (English Standard Version). Copyright, 2001 by Crossway, a publishing ministry of Good News Publishers.

Other references are from the Authorized King James Version and are annotated as such.

Edited by: Georgia Akers

Cover and Interior Layout: Dana Cline @ dclinedesign

Cover Art: Fred and Rene Hege

Printed in the United States of America

ISBN 978-1-952025-83-9

Give 'em JESUS!

1 Peter 3:15

[15]but in your hearts honor Christ the Lord as holy, always being prepared to make a defense to anyone who asks you for a reason for the hope that is in you; yet do it with gentleness and respect,

Jonah 3:1-3

[1]Then the word of the Lord came to Jonah the second time, saying, [2]"Arise, go … " [3]So Jonah arose and went …

Jim B.   Ride Share Operator — Las Vegas, NV

My relationship with the Lord Jesus began on September 17, 1977. Since that moment, I have always had a burden to be an effective witness for the Lord. However, lately, I have struggled to lay aside my fears and share the Gospel message with others. When I first met Fred Hege in November of 2021, he invited me to accompany him to share the Gospel on the Las Vegas Strip. Before we began, Fred gave a short inspirational lesson on how to apply The 4 Easy Steps for Sharing the Gospel in 4 Minutes. Almost immediately, I developed a comfort level in sharing the Gospel and leading others to Christ. I have experienced the joy of witnessing others come to the knowledge of God's saving grace. It is the most exciting experience a believer can ever have. I use The 4 Easy Steps every day in my rideshare business. Thank you, Fred, for helping me grow into a better witness and evangelist.

DEDICATION

This book is dedicated to Jesus Christ, my personal Lord and Savior and, to His church, the body of Christ. Thank you, pastors around the world who serve so faithfully. Many of you have shared with me what a high priority you subscribe to personal witness training and evangelism in your church. But, a shortage of funds, resources and available hours demand the deferral of training necessary to develop these skills. This book is also dedicated to you and to your church.

To you men and women of God who strive for compliance to God's call to be "fishers of men," this book is for you. To the one whose life is changed, to God be the glory!

CONTENTS

INTRODUCTION

When we speak of **soul winning**, we are explicitly engaging people for the purpose of leading them to the saving knowledge of Jesus Christ, so they may put their faith and trust solely in His shed blood for the remission of their sins. It is the responsibility of every child of God to be a witness for Christ. That command, not recommendation, was given over and over again throughout the New Testament. Here are just a few of the verses:

Matthew 28:19, 20 — *[19]"**Go** therefore and make disciples of all nations, baptizing them in the name of the Father and of the Son and of the Holy Spirit, [20]teaching them to observe all that I have commanded you. And behold, I am with you always, to the end of the age."*

Mark 16:15 — *[15]And he said to them, "**Go** into all the world and proclaim the gospel to the whole creation.*

Acts 1:8 — *[8]But **you will receive power** when the Holy Spirit has come upon you, and **you will be my witnesses** in Jerusalem and in all Judea and Samaria, and to the end of the earth."*

Jesus was speaking to His Forever Family and telling **us** that we are empowered by the Holy Spirit. It is **our responsibility** to witness for Christ. Every child of God should have a burning desire within them to share with others the wonderful truth of God's love, mercy and grace to condemned sinners. When that desire exists, there should be no need for coercion to get us out of our comfort zones.

We must remember, witnessing is not a debate or a contest, but simply presenting a cost/benefit analysis of making Jesus Christ Lord and Savior of your life to a lost sinner. At the end of the day, it is our responsibility as God's people to carry this message of the cross to our lost and dying world.

Do you know that 95% of born-again believers have never led one person to Christ? Unfortunately, 83% of new believers are led to Christ through personal witnessing. So, 95% of God's people are not engaged in the primary means God uses to win the lost in our day, one-on-one, conversational evangelism. In a recent survey by Barna Group, unbelievers were asked, "Would you be willing to listen to a gospel presentation from someone **passionate about their faith**?" 70% responded "Yes." Are you ready?

The purpose of this book is to equip every child of God with a personal witnessing skill set that you can adapt to your own personality type. As you witness the power of God's Word explode in the life of that lost sinner time after time, you will experience an excitement the likes of which you have never experienced before. As you step out of your comfort zone to make this presentation of the Gospel, you will develop confidence in the power of God's Word. In short order, your skill set will morph into a personal witnessing mindset at which point you become personal witnessing "intentional." You will actively seek new opportunities to share Jesus!

So, how are we going to do this? It's simple!

- First, I will introduce a methodology using The 5 Undeniable Truths found in Scripture that constitute a compelling presentation of the Gospel.
- Second, I will lay out a plan that I call "4 Easy Steps for Sharing the Gospel in 4 Minutes."
- Third, a 10-second approach for emergencies.
- Fourth, we will look at how to overcome the most common obstacles and objections you will face.
- Fifth, we will look at today's most common false doctrines and cults for a better understanding.
- Sixth, 13 types of people we will encounter and how to address them specifically with Scripture.
- Lastly, I will share a few parting thoughts.

Give 'em Jesus is by no means all that there is to know about being an effective witness for Christ. I have designed it to be conveniently carried at all times as a learning resource and help to get you started comfortably with sharing the Gospel. Winning the lost to Christ is challenging, but the rewards are out of this world! Remember, God does not hold us accountable for how much fruit we harvest. Our accountability is for faithfulness in sowing the seeds of the Gospel. He is Lord of the harvest — always!! Let's get started!

CHAPTER 1

HOW TO PRESENT THE GOSPEL

Before we discuss how to present the Gospel, let us first discuss what the Gospel is and what it is **not**. Many people genuinely believe in reaching others with the Gospel, but when their definition of the Gospel or their presentation of the Gospel is incompatible with Scripture, they are not accomplishing anything of eternal value. The word "Gospel" literally means "good news." What good news? Well, the Bible defines the Good News of the Gospel for us.

> ### 1 Corinthians 15:1-4
> *[1]Now I would remind you, brothers, of the Gospel I preached to you, which you received, in which you stand, [2]and by which you are being saved, if you hold fast to the word I preached to you — unless you believed in vain. [3]For I delivered to you as of first importance what I also received: that Christ died for our sins in accordance with the Scriptures, [4]that he was buried, that he was raised on the third day in accordance with the Scriptures.*

The Gospel is not simply a message of passing "from unbelief to belief." We need to ensure that we do not fall victim to sharing a diluted or polluted message of the Gospel. Some share a diluted message of God's love without God's condemnation of sin. Others share a diluted message of God's wrath and anger with the wicked without expressing God's grace and mercy that poured out love on Calvary. Still, others share a diluted Gospel without expressing the need for a sinner to repent and trust Christ by faith. Many cults of our day simply pollute the Gospel with a works-based performance for salvation.

In contrast, Paul says, " ... the Gospel ... according to the Scriptures" teaches:

- Christ died
- For our sins
- Was buried
- Rose again on the third day

This is the Biblical definition of the Gospel that one must put their faith and trust in for salvation. It is critically important that we ground our personal witnessing skill set on a clear and compelling presentation of this Gospel. It must be God's Gospel or it's no Gospel.

Colossians 4:3-4
³At the same time, pray also for us, that God may open to us a door for the word, to declare the mystery of Christ, on account of which I am in prison — ⁴that I may make it clear, which is how I ought to speak.

As we take time to study this critical subject of soul winning, ask the Holy Spirit to be your instructor in bringing God's wisdom and truth. Pray that He will guide every word and thought when we present the Gospel to others. We need His guidance and His help because it is the Holy Spirit, not the man of God, that must convict the sinner of his sin.

For where there is no conviction, there is no conversion. A salvation that you can talk a lost sinner into is a salvation Satan, most assuredly, will talk him out of!

Every soul winner must rely on the Holy Spirit, not their experience or proficiency.

> *John 6:44, 65*
> [44]*No one can come to me unless the Father who sent me draws him. And I will raise him up on the last day.*
> [65]*And he said, "This is why I told you that no one can come to me unless it is granted him by the Father."*

Let's examine The 5 Undeniable Truths essential for an effective presentation of the Gospel.

THE 5 UNDENIABLE TRUTHS APPROACH

Undeniable Truth #1: We Are All Sinners.

Until a person understands their condition, they cannot understand their position before a holy God. It is impossible for someone to trust by faith in the finished work of Jesus Christ when they have not acknowledged their condition without him. It is impossible to be forgiven until you first acknowledge that you need forgiveness. Any person that is saved *to something* (the Lord Jesus Christ) has to be saved *from something* (sin).

Why did Jesus shed His blood? It was not to provide us a home in Heaven. He shed His blood to forgive us of our sins. When someone accepts the forgiveness of sin, a home in Heaven is the result. Do not confuse the result with the reason. Jesus said he came into the world, not to condemn the world, but to save the world from the condemnation that already existed because of sin.

John 3:17
[17]For God did not send his Son into the world to condemn the world, but in order that the world might be saved through him.

In John 8, when the Pharisees brought the adulterous woman before Jesus, he saved her life but told her to go and sin no more. In Mark 2, when the lame man was brought to Him by four friends, Jesus first told the young man his sins were forgiven. Only after the Pharisees caused a scene did he tell the young man to rise up and walk. The adulterous woman desired to live, and the lame man preferred to walk. Christ focused on their sin, though he did help their condition. Everyone may want to go to Heaven; however, until they've received the forgiveness of their sins, they can't.

Definitions of sin

- Sin is anything we do to displease God.
- Sin is anything that violates the laws of God. This includes attitudes and actions.

VERSES ABOUT SIN

Romans 3:10
¹⁰as it is written: "None are righteous, no, not one ... "

Explanation: Not one person can claim to be righteous before a Holy God. Righteousness is the absence of unrighteousness. It is perfection. The problem is getting people to understand that we are "bad enough" to be condemned.

Ecclesiastes 7:20
²⁰Surely there is not a righteous man on earth who does good and never sins.

Explanation: Everyone who has ever lived on this earth is guilty of at least one violation of God's law. At least one small, seemingly, insignificant lie. It doesn't take a serial killer to be a sinner, just one small sin.

Romans 3:23
²³for all have sinned and fall short of the glory of God,

Explanation: The measuring stick for whether a person is "good enough" is the Lord Jesus Christ. He is the glory of God. No one measures up to Him. We all come short. It is all about how do you compare to "the glory of God," Jesus?

Psalm 51:5
⁵Behold, I was brought forth in iniquity, and in sin did my mother conceive me.

Explanation: We are all born with an inherent capacity to sin. No one has to teach a child how to lie. We all have that natural ability. We are born sinners.

Romans 5:12
¹²Therefore, just as sin came into the world through one man, and death through sin, and so death spread to all men because all sinned.

Explanation: Sin entered into this world with Adam's disobedience to God. The result was alienation from God and the curse of death. As descendants of Adam, we are born under this same curse and sin nature.

1 John 1:8
⁸If we say we have no sin, we deceive ourselves, and the truth is not in us.

Explanation: A person who says they are not a sinner is deceiving themself. An alcoholic who will not acknowledge they are one cannot be helped. An addict who will not acknowledge they are one cannot be helped. A sinner who will not acknowledge they are one cannot be saved.

1 John 1:10
[10]If we say we have not sinned, we make him a liar, and his word is not in us.

Explanation: For someone to say they are not a sinner is to call God a liar. God has declared that we are all sinners, and for us to refute that is to prove His Word does not dwell in us. A person who will not accept their sinful condition cannot accept Christ as their Savior. If a person will not acknowledge their sinful condition before a holy God, you cannot proceed with the Gospel. How will they accept the truth to come if they have not first accepted the truth given? The acknowledgment of sin is the foundation upon which the rest of the Gospel must be built.

Undeniable Truth #2:
There is a price for sin.

Just as it is impossible to present the Gospel without presenting that each and every person is a sinner, it is impossible to present sin without presenting the penalty. Once a person understands they are a sinner, they also need to understand that with their sin comes a debt and a required payment. Though people may be moved by the love of God, it is imperative they understand the condemnation to Hell that comes because of their sin. A sinner needs to admit they deserve punishment for their sins.

We make a mistake when we tell people the price for sin is simply "separation from God." Are they separated from God? Yes, but where are they separated, and for how long? They are separated from a holy God in a lake of fire for all eternity. Jesus showed His concern in this matter because He talked more about Hell than he did Heaven. He knew that people needed to know the full weight and payment for their sin.

If there is no severe consequence for severe action, there is no need to change. There is no need to accept Christ as Savior if there is no punishment for the sin that sent Him to the cross. Personal responsibility may not be popular in our world, but it is still a scriptural principle that we hold responsibility for our sin before God. People must understand the severe, everlasting punishment for sin. If they do not understand the weight of the penalty of sin, they will not be able to fully comprehend what Christ had to suffer to pay for the sins of the whole world.

Definition of sin's penalty

Our sin will separate us from God in a lake of fire called Hell for all eternity.

VERSES ABOUT SIN'S PENALTY

Romans 6:23
23For the wages of sin is death, but the free gift of God is eternal life in Christ Jesus our Lord.

Explanation: The word *"wages"* denotes an earned payment. The reason for the payment and the extent of the payment are included in this verse. The reason for this wage is *"sin,"* and the extent of the payment is *"death."* This is just.

Illustration: Everyone who works a job expects their wages in the form of a paycheck. It is reasonable and just to expect that if you have worked the hours, you receive compensation for that labor. It is just as reasonable for God to compensate our sin with a wage of death. We committed them; now we receive the full payment for them.

Hebrews 9:27
27And just as it is appointed for man to die once, and after that comes judgment,

Explanation: Everyone is going to die once, 100% of the time. Guaranteed! That is just a fact of life. However, once we die, there is a judgment for the sins we have committed.

Revelation 21:8
8But as for the cowardly, the faithless, the detestable, as for murderers, the sexually immoral, sorcerers, idolaters, and all liars, their portion will be in the lake that burns with fire and sulfur, which is the second death."

Explanation: God gives us a long list of sins to which we would give different weights. We would classify *"murderers"* as much worse than *"liars,"* but before a perfect, holy God, they are both worthy of condemnation. The lake of fire is an everlasting punishment for sin, which the Bible describes as the *"second death."* Though we will all die physically, this death is temporary. It is temporary because the pain of death is gone when the believer takes their last breath. The second death is everlasting. The pain and suffering of that death will last throughout all eternity.

> **Matthew 25:41**
> [41] *"Then he will say to those on his left, 'Depart from me, you cursed, into the eternal fire prepared for the devil and his angels ... ' "*

Explanation: When someone breaks the laws of our city or nation, we say they are on the *"wrong side of the law."* Here, Jesus explains that every person who stands before God, still bearing the weight of their sins, will be on the wrong side of God's throne. He will look at those whose sins are unconfessed and condemn them to the same fiery judgment that the devil and his angels are condemned.

What would you do if you woke up tonight to find your house was on fire? Would you run for the front door and hope everyone else got out safe? Or, would you be concerned about whether or not everyone was getting a good night's sleep? The answer to both of these is NO! You would wake up everyone in the house and do your best to get everyone out. We have the same responsibility to that lost and dying world around us. They are asleep in their sin, and a great, terrible fire is quickly approaching.

In Luke 16, we find the factual account of the rich man and Lazarus. The rich man was asleep in his wealth and sufficiency, but there came a day when death awakened him. When he woke up, he was already in Hell. It was too late for him to realize the error of his way, but he quickly turned his focus to his brothers still alive on this earth. He pleaded for someone to go back and warn them of the punishment to come. No one would warn the lost more of the punishment of sin that is to come than someone already in Hell. They can't. So, we have to!

The Bible tells us that some people are only motivated to salvation because of the fear of Hell.

Jude verse 23
[23]*save others by snatching them out of the fire; to others show mercy with fear, hating even the garment stained by the flesh.*

We need to yell, **"FIRE!"**

Undeniable Truth #3: Christ has already paid the price for our sin.

A message of condemnation without a message of hope isn't worth sharing. Once a person has acknowledged their sinful condition and admitted they deserve to pay for their own sins, they are ready to hear that Christ already paid the price. This is why the Gospel is called the Good News. There is no better news for a prisoner condemned to death and headed to the death chamber than to hear the declaration of his pardon!

Once they have admitted their guilt, a person needs to understand that Christ took upon Himself their punishment and that of the whole world. They need to understand the suffering of the Lord Jesus Christ for our sins. If they understand this, they will realize how seriously God takes sin and its punishment. They also need to know that Christ did not die for the good but the sinful. He did not wait until men got good enough to deserve His sacrifice. He gave Himself in spite of our sin.

Romans 5:8
8but God shows his love for us in that while we were still sinners, Christ died for us.

An important point that should be made with this verse is that the reference to God and Christ is in harmony with Christ's deity as God. Now is an excellent time to press the point that Jesus is God, and He has always been God. John 1:1-3 is probably the best and most straightforward passage of Scripture to support this point. If a sinner does not believe that Jesus is the sinless Son of God, then they cannot truly put their faith in the shed blood of Jesus for the forgiveness of their sin. Only God has the right to forgive trespasses against Him. If they do not believe that Jesus is God, then they don't believe He forgives.

We must also help the lost comprehend what all our sin did to Jesus.

1. Jesus took our place of suffering and shame.
2. Jesus paid the penalty of an everlasting Hell.
3. Jesus, who is without sin, became our sin in order to pay the price for it.
4. Jesus was separated from the Father because of our sin.
5. Jesus shed His blood as the price for all sin.

Definition of Christ's payment

Jesus became our sin and paid for it by shedding His sinless blood on the cross.

VERSES ABOUT CHRIST'S PAYMENT

1 Peter 3:18 — Jesus took our place of suffering and shame.

18For Christ also suffered once for sins, the righteous for the unrighteous, that he might bring us to God, being put to death in the flesh but made alive in the spirit,

Explanation: Jesus hung on the cross in open shame and excruciating agony because of our sin. We deserved to be scourged, spit upon and nailed to our own cross, and mocked while upon it. Yet, Jesus took upon Himself all of this suffering and shame. He took our place to pay for our sins.

Isaiah 53:11 — Jesus paid the penalty of an everlasting hell.

> *[11]Out of the anguish of his soul he shall see and be satisfied; by his knowledge shall the righteous one, my servant, make many to be accounted righteous, and he shall bear their iniquities.*

Explanation: Jesus had to suffer more than just a physical death on a cross to pay for our sins. Jesus paid the full penalty of an everlasting lake of fire for the entire world — past, present and future. His suffering was unimaginable.

2 Corinthians 5:21 — Jesus, who is without sin, became our sin in order to pay for it.

> *[21]For our sake he made him to be sin who knew no sin, so that in him we might become the righteousness of God.*

Explanation: It would be impossible for a sinner to pay for the sins of others because they would be under the condemnation of their own sin. The only reason Jesus could pay the price for our sin is because He was without sin.

Matthew 27:46 — Jesus was separated from the Father because of our sin

> *[46]And about the ninth hour Jesus cried out with a loud voice, saying, "Eli, Eli, lema sabachthani?" that is, "My God, my God, why have you forsaken me?"*

Explanation: Jesus had never known separation from the Father. Just as Jesus cried out in agony from the solitary suffering of the cross, every sinner who dies without Christ will cry out in suffering, separated from God.

Hebrews 13:12 — Jesus shed His blood as the price for sin

> *[12]So Jesus also suffered outside the gate in order to sanctify the people through his own blood.*

Explanation: The Bible makes it clear that the price for sin is blood. It was not the death of Christ that paid for our sins. It was His sinless blood as the Son of God that the Bible emphasizes and so must we.

VERSES ABOUT THE BLOOD

Romans 5:9
[9]Since, therefore, we have now been justified by his blood, much more shall we be saved by him from the wrath of God.

Ephesians 2:13
[13]But now in Christ Jesus you who once were far off have been brought near by the blood of Christ.

Hebrews 9:22
[22]Indeed, under the law almost everything is purified with blood, and without the shedding of blood there is no forgiveness of sins.

Romans 3:25
[5]whom God put forward as a propitiation by

his blood, to be received by faith. This was to show God's righteousness, because in his divine forbearance he had passed over former sins.

Undeniable Truth #4:
God's free gift offer.

A key point in the presentation of the Gospel is that the eternal and everlasting life offered by God is a free gift. There is nothing anyone is required to do to obtain or retain the gift of salvation that God offers. Works-based merit is a primary error of most other religions and cults. They teach that a person must either earn salvation through works and/or retain salvation through works. Neither of those teachings is a Scriptural truth. A gift requires nothing before or after the receiving of it.

If God required something in return for salvation, it would not be a gift. The Bible, however, calls it the "gift of God." The only requirement for a gift is that you receive it.

Definition of God's free gift

God offers the gift of everlasting life to all those who will simply put their faith and trust in the price Jesus paid for our sins on the cross. No works are required.

VERSES ABOUT GOD'S FREE GIFT

One of the best verses to apply for explaining this point is one that almost everyone is acquainted with, John 3:16.

> ### John 3:16
> *(1) For God (2) so loved (3) the world, (4) that he gave his only Son, (5) that whoever believes in him (6) should not perish (7) but have eternal life.*

Explanation: This verse explains God's free gift so thoroughly that you may not need to go to other Scriptures. Below is a breakdown of this verse that can help you explain God's free gift of everlasting and eternal life.

1. The provider of the gift: *"For God ... "*

The only one who could offer a gift of this magnitude is God. He is, also, the only one who can truly offer a gift without any strings attached. We may give gifts that are not earned; however, we always expect something in return, even if it is just a "thank you." We give gifts to our children, but we want to enjoy the smiles on their faces. We give gifts to our friends, but if we do not hear of their gratefulness or thankfulness, we sometimes feel that our gift was unappreciated. God has no selfish motive in offering His free gift of eternal life. He is only concerned about our eternal destination.

2. The motive of the gift: *" ... so loved ... "*

God's motivation had nothing at all to do with man's actions; it just had to do with man. **God so loved.** The motivation behind His gift of everlasting life was His deep, abiding love for man. Consequently, there is nothing a man has to do to earn it. Many people question the love of God because bad things happen; however, there is no greater evidence for the fact that *"God is love" (1 John 4:8)* than the proof of love He showed by sending the Lord Jesus Christ to die on the cross of Calvary. He did this, not because He was required to or was obligated to, but simply because He *"so loved."*

3. The benefactor of the gift: *"… the world, … "*

God does not offer this gift to the animals, trees or any other part of His creation. God offers this gift to mankind. What love this shows! Out of all God's creation, man is the only one who has broken God's laws and is guilty of sin. Yet, God presented His love to guilty men through Jesus' broken body on the cross. The cross is proof that God's gift is free and without requirement, because He chose us, the least worthy, to offer His gift of life.

4. The price of the gift: *"… that he gave his only Son, … "*

Every gift costs the giver something. Whether it is their time, talent or treasure, the gift costs something. God gave His free gift by paying an invaluable price. The shed blood of His son, Jesus Christ, was the price He paid for our gift.

5. The requirement of the gift: *" ... that whoever believes in Him ... "*

There is only one requirement that God puts on His free gift of eternal life. A lost sinner must put their faith in Jesus' blood to receive the gift.

6. The necessity of the gift: *" ... should not perish, ... "*

We may receive gifts on this earth that we really don't need. However, there is no greater need that we have than to be rescued from the condemnation of Hell. God's free gift provides the only way of escape. His gift is the life preserver thrown to the drowning soul who has fallen into the raging sea. It is their only hope, and He is ours.

7. The result of the gift: *" ... but have eternal life."*

The result and extent of this gift of "life" is seen in the word *"everlasting."* Everlasting means that there is a beginning *(the moment I receive the gift)*, but there is absolutely no ending *(it lasts throughout all eternity)*. The gifts we give and receive on this earth are temporal, but God's gift, that He offers freely, is everlasting.

Romans 5:8
8but God shows his love for us in that while we were still sinners, Christ died for us.

Explanation: God **exhibited** or **showed** how much He loved us. Notice that this verse tells us that He demonstrated His love *"while we were still sinners."* God did not require man to get better before He showed His love. Christ died for us when we didn't deserve it. It's free.

> ***Ephesians 2:8-9***
> *⁸For by grace you have been saved through faith. And this is not your own doing; it is the gift of God, ⁹not a result of works, so that no one may boast.*

Explanation: The *"gift of God,"* which is His grace, is received through faith in the price Jesus paid for our sins by shedding His blood on the cross. We are told in verse nine that God's gift of gracious salvation is *"not of works."* For, if it were of works, man would have a reason to *"boast."* No flesh shall glory, or *"boast,"* in His presence. *(1 Corinthians 1:29)*

Undeniable Truth #5: Faith in Christ is the only way.

A lost person needs to know that their faith must be in Christ alone for the forgiveness of their sins. To trust in Christ plus something else, is to trust in the something else. They must put their complete faith in the finished work of Jesus Christ to forgive them of their debt of sin. They must trust His blood to cleanse them.

Definitions of faith in Christ

- You must put your faith and trust in the

blood of Jesus to forgive your sins.

- Your faith must be in the finished work of Jesus Christ *(His death, burial and resurrection)*, plus nothing and minus nothing.

VERSES ABOUT FAITH IN CHRIST

John 14:6

⁶Jesus said to him, "I am the way, and the truth, and the life. No one comes to the Father except through me."

Explanation: This is the most explicit statement that Jesus could have possibly used to define Himself. "The" is the definitive article, meaning "the one and only." Jesus said He is the one and only way, the one and only truth, and the one and only life. To be able to come to the Father *(enter Heaven)*, you must go through Jesus alone.

Galatians 2:16

¹⁶yet we know that a person is not justified by works of the law but through faith in Jesus Christ, so we also have believed in Christ Jesus, in order to be justified by faith in Christ and not by works of the law, because by works of the law no one will be justified.

Explanation: The only way to be *"justified"* in God's eyes is through faith in Jesus Christ. No work could do that. In the eyes of God, Jesus makes me "just-if-ied never sinned."

Philippians 3:9
⁹and be found in him, not having a
righteousness of my own that comes from the
law, but that which comes through faith in
Christ, the righteousness from God that depends
on faith ...

Explanation: We have already covered how
Jesus is the measuring stick of righteousness.
Righteousness does not come through the law.
Righteousness comes *"through faith in Christ."*

1 John 5:11, 12
¹¹And this is the testimony, that God gave
us eternal life, and this life is in his Son.
¹²Whoever has the Son has life; whoever does
not have the Son of God does not have life.

Explanation: This is perhaps the most explicit
definition of salvation in all of Scripture. If you
have trusted Jesus Christ, the Son, you have
life. If you have not trusted Jesus Christ, you
are spiritually lost and condemned. Salvation
hangs upon faith in Jesus Christ alone.

The Moment of Decision!

**At this point, you are ready to bring
the person to a place of decision.**

Our friend must make a decision from 2 choices:

**1. Reject the message of the Gospel
and go their own way.**

If a person is unwilling to accept what the

Word of God says about them and Jesus, you cannot continue. We have a responsibility to move on to someone else.

> ***Ezekiel 33:9***
> *⁹But if you warn the wicked to turn from his way, and he does not turn from his way, that person shall die in his iniquity, but you will have delivered your soul.*

2. Accept the message of the Gospel and trust Christ.

If the person is ready and willing to accept the message of the Gospel you have just shared with them, then take them back through a brief 1-2 minute review. When reviewing the Gospel, briefly ask them for a response of acceptance or denial.

Example of Gospel Review

"Let me just review with you for a moment to make sure you understand and see if you have any questions."

Truth #1: *"Do you understand and agree with God's Word that you are a sinner?"*

Truth #2: *"Do you understand and agree with God's Word that, because of your sin, you deserve punishment in the lake of fire for eternity?"*

Truth #3: *"Do you understand and agree with God's Word that Jesus paid the price for your sin and took your punishment?"*

Truth #4: *"Do you understand and agree with God's Word that God has offered the blood of Jesus to you as a free gift in payment for your sins?"*

Truth #5: *"Do you understand and agree with God's Word that you must put your faith in Jesus' blood alone to cleanse you and forgive you of your sins?"*

Having confirmed their understanding and acceptance of the Gospel ask,

"Would you be willing, right now, to pray and tell the Lord Jesus Christ that you want to put your faith and trust in what He did to forgive you of your sins?"

NOTE: The best way to have someone accept Christ as their Savior is for them to pray their own prayer in their own words. Share Romans 10:9-13 with them:

Romans 10:9-13

[9]because, if you confess with your mouth that Jesus is Lord and believe in your heart that God raised him from the dead, you will be saved. [10]For with the heart one believes and is justified, and with the mouth one confesses and is saved. [11]For the Scripture says, "Everyone who believes in him will not be put to shame." [12]For there is no distinction between Jew and Greek; for the same Lord is Lord of all, bestowing his riches on all who call on him. [13]For "everyone who calls on the name of the Lord will be saved."

Explanation: It is not the words of a prayer that save a person. **Emphasize this point! It is faith in the shed blood of Jesus that one confesses to God with that brings salvation.**

"With the heart," not with the head, man receives Christ by faith. *"Why don't you just bow your head and pray to Jesus? Tell Him that you know you are a sinner, deserve to spend eternity in a lake of fire, accept His blood for the payment of your sins, and trust only Him to save your soul."*

Example of a Sinner's Prayer

"God, from my heart, I admit to You that I am a sinner and I ask for Your forgiveness. I believe that Your Son, Jesus, took the punishment I deserve in the lake of fire for all eternity by shedding His blood on the cross. He gave His life as the full payment for my sins and rose again from the dead. Thank you for changing my heart. I now confess and turn from my sins and receive Your Son, Jesus, as my Savior and Lord. Amen!"

NOTE: There are occasions, such as with multiple individuals, where I use what I call "The Great Confession" congruent with Romans 10:9-13. Have them repeat after you.

"I believe that Jesus is the Christ, the Son of the living God. Who died for my sins: past, present and future — 100% of the time. And I confess Him as my personal Lord and Savior."

If you do this, again, emphasize that it is not the words of any prayer or confession that saves. It is the faith they present to God from their heart.

NOTE: When they finish praying, you need to ask them some questions to ensure they know, once again, that the prayer had to come from their heart.

"When you prayed that prayer or confession just now, did you mean what you said?"

"Did you pray or confess with faith, believing that Jesus will save you if you just ask Him?"

"Now, on a scale of 0%-100%, how certain are you that if you die today, you would spend eternity in Heaven?"

The Assurance They Now Have in Christ!

Once a person has accepted the message of salvation, our job is not yet finished. They need to understand the security and assurance they now have in Jesus Christ. We need to teach them about the "security of the believer." They cannot lose salvation. Christ not only died to save them from their sins, but He also rose again to give them victory over the power of sin in our life. Because He lives, He has the power to keep me.

Definitions of assurance of salvation

- Whether we die today, tomorrow or in a hundred years, Jesus has promised that He will never leave or forsake us when we receive Him.

- There is nothing I can do as a child of God that will ever cause my heavenly Father to remove me from His "Forever Family."

VERSES ABOUT THE ASSURANCE OF SALVATION

John 5:24

24Truly, truly, I say to you, whoever hears my word and believes him who sent me has eternal life. He does not come into judgment, but has passed from death to life.

Explanation: When we put our faith in Christ, we pass from death into life. Just as Jesus died and came to life to live forever, we also have that kind of life.

1 John 5:13

13I write these things to you who believe in the name of the Son of God, that you may know that you have eternal life.

Explanation: The key word in this verse is *"know."* When people put faith in Jesus' finished work for their salvation, they do not have to "hope so" about their eternity. They can *"know"* so, with **100%** certainty! He promised, and I trust Him.

Hebrews 13:5

*5Keep your life free from love of money, and be content with what you have, **for He has said, "I will never leave you nor forsake you."***

Explanation: You can't get any clearer than this. When Jesus, the *"He"* of this verse, said *"never,"* He meant *"never."* Not only will He not leave me *(that deals with the loss of salvation)*, but He also said He would not forsake me *(that deals with the provision and care of His children after salvation)*.

John 10:28-30
28" ... I give them eternal life, and they will never perish, and no one will snatch them out of my hand. 29My Father, who has given them to me, is greater than all, and no one is able to snatch them out of the Father's hand. 30I and the Father are one."

Explanation: Jesus is the one who gives *"eternal life"*; therefore, He is the only one who could take it away. He has already promised that He would not do that. So, I can rest assured in the salvation He gives. Jesus also said in this passage that *"no man"* can pluck us out of His or the Father's hand. *"No man"* would include me, another person or Satan. When we trust Christ, we *"shall never perish."*

Ephesians 1:12, 13
12so that we who were the first to hope in Christ might be to the praise of his glory. 13In him you also, when you heard the word of truth, the Gospel of your salvation, and believed in him, were sealed with the promised Holy Spirit, ...

Explanation: We are saved by the hands of the Son, sealed by the hands of the Spirit and secured by the hands of the Father.

> ***Romans 8:38, 39***
> *38For I am sure that neither death nor life, nor angels nor rulers, nor things present nor things to come, nor powers, 39nor height nor depth, nor anything else in all creation, will be able to separate us from the love of God in Christ Jesus our Lord.*

Explanation: Absolutely nothing can separate us from the salvation God gives.

Once they understand their security in Christ, you've thoroughly presented the Gospel.

CHAPTER 1

CHAPTER 2

4 EASY STEPS FOR SHARING THE GOSPEL IN 4 MINUTES

If the only tool in your toolbox is a hammer, then all of your problems will look like nails. If The 5 Undeniable Truths is the only tool in your soul winner's toolbox, then all of your witnessing opportunities will require 30 minutes. This is a tactical, planned engagement witnessing tool. Although it is a thorough presentation, we may not have that much time. We need an additional, more versatile tool, that we can apply to the many shorter windows of opportunity we encounter each day. We need a tool for blue collar evangelism. We must prepare ourselves for soul winning moments that emerge "in the trenches" unexpectedly every day. Expanding our toolbox will better equip us to reach more people. For those of us who live in the "fast lane," 4 Easy Steps for Sharing the Gospel in 4 Minutes might be a more practical tool. Let's examine it!

Step 1 — The Engagement Question

Jesus is the master communicator. One of His most passionate encounters is with the Samaritan woman at the well. (John 4:1-38) Here He demonstrates Jesus-style evangelism in its purest form. There are several fundamental principles of which we must take special note.

One, Jesus initiates the conversation with an Engagement Question, "May I have a drink of water?" Jesus demonstrated that it is our responsibility to engage the lost sinner. The lost sinner, in most cases, will have an aversion to the things of God, to God's people, to the Church and to the Word of God. In many cases, they will never come through our church doors. Jesus said, "**Go** into Judea, Samaria and to the uttermost parts of the world." About 83% of new believers come to Christ through one-on-one evangelism. Church services, crusades, special events, etc., comprise the other 17%, which require them coming to us. Because of their aversion, we must carry the message of the cross to them! After all, if we as God's people don't do it, who is going to do it for us? Nobody!

Secondly, the Engagement Question is of critical importance for another reason. Jesus was demonstrating that the man of God must always be in control of the conversation. Yes, he must be a good listener, by all means, but always in control of the direction of the conversation. The adulteress lady tried to change the subject of the conversation with Jesus from her immoral lifestyle to where those in her country should worship God. Jesus brings her back to the purpose of revealing himself as the Messiah. He identifies himself as "The One" who can provide "living water" and the forgiveness of sin.

So, Jesus initiates the conversation and ensures that the conversation stays on target, her recognizing Him as Messiah.

Thirdly, the Engagement Question is critically important because this is where we establish our comfort level for the entire presentation. Our lost friends can sense when we are comfortable and in control. It gives them assurance that we are genuine and sincere. Remember, Barna Group asked a group of unbelievers, "Would you be willing to listen to a presentation of the Gospel from someone **passionate about their faith**?" 70% said they would listen! They are looking for our message. They can sense sincerity or the lack thereof. When we demonstrate passion and sincerity, they develop a comfort level with us. They want to hear more!

So, what does your Engagement Question need to be? It can be anything you want it to be. In Appendix 1, page 135, you will find a list of Engagement Questions with which you might identify. You may even want to tailor your own Engagement Question. It doesn't matter as long as you feel comfortable in the application. I have seen many powerful men and women of God who are incredibly effective soul winners use an Engagement Question that I would feel most uncomfortable applying. Does that mean they should adopt a different Engagement Question? Of course not! They have obviously found a comfort level with an Engagement Question that initiates their path to the Give 'em Jesus Scriptures. In personal witnessing, one size never fits all. The methodology that Jesus lays out for us does fit all. So, we will work inside this Jesus-style personal witnessing framework and adopt a skill set that we can mold to fit our individual personality type.

Having applied the Engagement Question, we must wait for a response.

Illustration: One of my favorite Engagement Questions is, "Do you have a New Testament?" Or, "Do you have a copy of the Word of God?" Their response will generally be, "Yes, I do." or "No, I do not." Now, at this point, no matter what their response is, I have been successful in initiating a personal witness conversation. In about 15 seconds, I have accomplished everything that we outlined above.

Step 2 — Applying the Spiritual Thermometer

In Step 2, we are searching for the presence of the Holy Spirit. Occasionally, you will find that this presence is detectable with their response to the Engagement Question. They will, occasionally, give you information beyond a simple "Yes" or "No" answer voluntarily. If there is a detectable presence of the Holy Spirit, skip Step 2, and ask for permission to share the Give 'em Jesus Scriptures in Step 3.

ALWAYS, ALWAYS GET TO THE GIVE 'EM JESUS SCRIPTURES AS SOON AS POSSIBLE!

However, most commonly, the Holy Spirit's presence will not yet be detectable, in which case we proceed with Step 2, applying the Spiritual Thermometer. The Spiritual Thermometer serves two purposes.

First, the Spiritual Thermometer is a series of strategically designed questions that serve as a sensor enabling us to detect if the Holy Spirit is present. The Holy Spirit's presence is a requirement!

> ### John 6:44, 65
> **44No one can come to me unless the Father who sent me draws him.** And I will raise him up on the last day.
> 65And he said, "This is why I told you that **no one can come to me unless it is granted him by the Father.**"

After all, where there is no moving of the Holy Spirit, there is no decision for Jesus!

And second, if the Holy Spirit is present, the Spiritual Thermometer will frequently give us a measure of what magnitude and where the Holy Spirit is moving in this individual's life.

I have laid out a few options to help guide you in applying the Spiritual Thermometer. In Appendix 1, page 137, you will find 6 Spiritual Thermometer Questions. We can use one question or a series of these questions as time permits. I usually use 1-3 questions of my choice based on the circumstances at hand. Remember, this is a sensor process searching for the Holy Spirit's presence.

Illustration: "Do you have a New Testament?" (The Engagement Question)

"Yes." (Response but no indication of the Holy Spirit's presence)

"Do you have any spiritual beliefs?" (Spiritual Thermometer Question #1)

"Yes, I believe in God."

"OK, but do you believe in Jesus?" (Spiritual Thermometer Question #2)

"Yes."

"Who do you think Jesus was?" (Spiritual Thermometer Question #3)

"A really good man." (or prophet, or teacher, or theologian, etc.)

"Could I share a few verses that might give you some insight on who Jesus really was?" (Transition)

"Sure." (Presence of the Holy Spirit! Immediately apply the Give 'em Jesus Scriptures!)

"Would you please read this first verse?" (Pointing to John 3:16)

"For God so loved the world ..."

So, in approximately 1 minute, I successfully applied my Engagement Question but detected no indication of the Holy Spirit's presence. I applied 3 Spiritual Thermometer Questions and then found the presence of the Holy Spirit. This individual does believe in Jesus but does not precisely know who Jesus was. At this point, I ask permission to share the Give 'em Jesus Scriptures. I, now, have them holding my Testament and reading out loud (to them, to me, and to all who may be second-hand listeners)! All in about 1 minute, and I am right on target!

You might be asking, "Is it always this simple?" Of course not! I cannot always find that presence of the Holy Spirit for which I am looking. I may have to apply my Engagement Question to a multitude of people before I can find that individual who has the Holy Spirit's presence. But, here's the deal, when I am able to detect the Holy Spirit's presence, from my experience, the dialogue that I have outlined above results in a decision for Jesus about 80% of the time! The power is in detecting the Holy Spirit's presence and then applying the Give 'em Jesus Scriptures!

Another important reason for carefully applying the Spiritual Thermometer is it aids as a filter in ensuring good stewardship of our time. In Colossians 4:3-6, as Paul prays for his witness opportunity in prison, he asks God that he might "walk in wisdom toward outsiders making the best use of his time." Time is always critical, and we want to make sure that we spend a disproportionate amount of our time with the lost and, more specifically, where there is a Holy Spirit presence. I cannot emphasize this enough. Otherwise, we may spend all day sowing in unfertile soil or witnessing to those who are already believers. Constrained by time with an ultimate goal to reach the lost, unwise stewardship of our time will diminish our productivity and effectiveness. Wise time stewardship was a concern of Paul's and should, also, be our concern.

Now, another application of the Spiritual Thermometer is through the use of the Acid Question, Appendix 1, page 137. Using the same engagement dialogue I used above, this application should go something like this.

Illustration: "Do you have a copy of the New Testament?" (The Engagement Question)

"Yes." (Response but no indication of the Holy Spirit's presence)

"Do you have any spiritual beliefs?" (Spiritual Thermometer Question #1)

"Yes, I believe in God."

"That's great! But, let me just ask you, what, for me is, the most important question that we must ask ourselves, 'On a scale of 0%-100%, how certain are you that if you die today, you would spend eternity in Heaven?'" (Dead silence while I wait for my friend's response to the Acid Question.)

If time is an issue or there are distractions, I may go straight to the Acid Question after the Engagement Question. But regardless, I will almost always apply the Acid Question, "On a scale of 0%-100%, how certain are you that if you die today, you would spend eternity in Heaven?" This response tells us much we need to know about the person we are witnessing to and gives us a quick, easy transition to the Give 'em Jesus Scriptures.

Categorically, we will get one of three answers:

- 0%
- 1%-99.9%
- 100%

A 0% Meter Reading

So, how do we interpret their response? First, let's look at the 0% individual. Sometimes this person will simply say "0%" and deny any thoughts of dying. We know from Scripture this individual is not telling the truth.

Ecclesiastes 3:11
11 ... He has put eternity into man's heart ...

Every individual thinks about dying and, most, at a very young age. This person is lying and evasive. We will ask permission to share the

Give 'em Jesus Scriptures, but they will most likely refuse. Frequently, this individual will refuse to take any of our resources, especially the Testament. Sometimes a gentle request to share the Scriptures a second time is warranted. However, if they refuse a second time, we move on without delay.

Other individuals who may meter at 0% are atheists, agnostics and Satanists, which comprise a broad group. Let's drill deeper! Atheists and agnostics will, generally, tell you they do not believe in Heaven and Hell. They will often profess to be atheist or agnostic when, in fact, all they want is for you to go away! Instead of politely saying, "I do not have any interest in discussing spiritual matters," posturing as an atheist is their means of saying, "Go away!" They intend to discourage and distract you.

I generally find honest professing atheists and agnostics divided into two categories. One, those atheists who truly believe there is no God and in some type of proverbial "Big Bang" theory or, in the case of the agnostics, that the human mind is incapable of comprehending God. Or, a second classification, those with hearts hardened by unfortunate circumstances such as disaster, misfortune, pain, suffering, the horrible death of a loved one, etc. They are quick to tell you that if a loving God existed, He would not permit things of this nature to occur. Some are trying to live in limbo. Their pain has distorted their view of God. Instead of unbelievers, they may just be suffering doubters. There is a huge difference!

Occasionally, I have had them tell me they are atheist and, after agreeing to an invitation to read the Give 'em Jesus Scriptures, make decisions for Jesus. If they, too, refuse the Scriptures, a gentle second invitation might be fruitful, but if denied, we move on. **We are never contentious** in our engagement!

As for the Satanists, they believe in Heaven and Hell, but with distorted conceptions. They have spiritual beliefs. They just worship the wrong god. They will, occasionally, take a copy of your Testament and agree to read it. If not now, maybe we can get a commitment to read the Give 'em Jesus Scriptures before bed with a follow-up phone call tomorrow. Sometimes, we are able to see these individuals come to a decision for Jesus. They may not look exactly like us, but I have established lasting relationships with some of these individuals. They are typically easier to engage than atheists and agnostics because they tend to be more open about their beliefs. While many proclaimed atheists and agnostics do not know what they believe, the Satanist does. Consequently, he is easier to engage.

There is a third group of individuals that randomly meters at 0%. It includes the person who has found complacency in their sin. They, frequently, will have a sin so deeply engrained for years or, maybe decades, that it has become an accepted lifestyle for them. Those entrenched in sexual sin as defined in the Word of God come to mind. The LGBTQ community occasionally falls into this 0% category. Frequently, they refuse the Scriptures.

Those addicted to substances, alcohol, porn, etc., sometimes fall into this category. However, I generally find them much more receptive to the Scriptures and willing to consider repentance and a relationship with Jesus as a last-ditch effort to find healing.

A fourth group that meters at 0% includes the person living under conviction of sin but doesn't know where or whom to turn in their search for truth. To this individual, you may be just the person they are searching for and do not know where to find. Searching for a message of hope and deliverance, they find comfort in the Give 'em Jesus Scriptures. The message of God's love and mercy enamors the heart of those searching for truth. Commonly, they are more than ready to make a decision for Jesus.

No matter who the individual is, and despite metering at 0%, we try to get them to the Give 'em Jesus Scriptures. If denied, sometimes a second appeal is warranted. If rejected a second time, we move on quickly, being good stewards of our time!

A 1%-99.9% Meter Reading

The second category of respondents to the Acid
Question includes those who respond, 1%-99.9%.
In this category, we have garnered a group of
individuals who definitely test Holy Spirit
positive. They have thought about their spiritual
eternity. They, generally, have a genuine concern
for their spiritual health. This category of
respondents is quick and ready to share with
you why they meter in this range. "I got out of
fellowship with God when I went to college."
"I fell on hard times because I lost my job;
consequently, I am not sure God loves me
anymore." "I got saved when I was younger,
but I have done some bad things, and maybe,
God has disqualified my salvation." "I made
that decision years ago when grandma took me
to church, but I stopped going as I got older."
And, the excuses behind their backslidden
condition could go on forever! Because they are
Holy Spirit positive, they have some concept of
Heaven, Hell and the Judgment. They are most
often receptive to the Scriptures, and from this
group, we can expect to see around 80% willing
to make that decision for Jesus or rededication.
Frequently, this group is enthusiastic about
becoming our brothers and sisters in Christ!

Sometimes, those who meter in the 1%-99.9%
category can also be somewhat resistant to
the Scriptures. In order to address them, let's
take inventory of what we know and do not

know. First, we know that they are Holy Spirit positive. Second, we know they do not have a 100% assurance of their faith, which is our goal. What we do not know is, what they are basing their partial assurance of salvation on. So, how do we get all of this cleared up?

Illustration: Is there something in your life that I can pray with you for today? (The Engagement Question)

"Yes. I am struggling with issues concerning my job."

"OK. But, first, let me ask you what, for me, is the single most important question that every person must ask themselves. On a scale of 0%-100%, how certain are you that if you die today, you would spend eternity in Heaven?" (Dead silence while I wait for my friend's response to the Acid Question.)

"I'd say around 75%."

"Hmmm... OK, interesting. What would you say you are basing the 75% on?" (The "Hmmm ... " factor telegraphs that I am listening intently.)

"Well, when I was 12 years old, grandma used to take me to church, and one Sunday morning, I responded to an invitation to receive Christ."

"Great! Were you sincere?"

"I thought I was at the time."

"OK, but what about the 25% assurance of

your salvation that you cannot account for today?"

"When I turned 16, I stopped going to church, and I have never pursued my relationship with God since."

"May I share some verses of Scripture that might give some insight into your concerns?" (Transition to the Give 'em Jesus Scriptures!)

"Sure."

"Would you read right here, please?" (Pointing to John 3:16)

The lynchpin in this scenario is, **"What about the 25% assurance of your salvation that you cannot account for today?"** Why? Because no matter what they are basing their 75% assurance on, they are by default living in defeat! (This will perpetuate job worries.) The 75% assurance of salvation may be predicated on a previous prayer of confession, grandma or mama's faith, striving to be a "good person," obeying the Ten Commandments, always striving to help other people or trusting in some other works-based performance for salvation. Perhaps, they are even basing their 75% assurance (or even 99.9%) on the shed blood of Jesus for the forgiveness of their sins, but regardless, they are still living in defeat, at least to some degree, without the 100% assurance. This is even by their own admission. Bottom line, we definitely do not want to leave this individual without their 100% assurance of salvation. Is this a reasonable expectation? According to the disciple John, it most definitely is!

> ### 1 John 5:13
> [13]*I write these things to you who believe in the name of the Son of God, that you may know that you have eternal life.*

We have God's promise that we can know with 100% assurance. You may ask, "Is this individual's name written in the Lamb's Book of Life?" The short answer is, we do not know because even they do not know, hence the 75% assurance. So, whether they got their salvation at grandma's church as a child or not is a risk that no one can afford to take! And furthermore, the most miserable man in the entire world is not the man who is spiritually lost. The most miserable man in the entire world is the born again believer who has drifted out of fellowship with God! Consequently, decisions for rededication and those for professing faith in Jesus for the first time are equally important! We need to make sure that everyone enjoys the peace of knowing Jesus Christ as their personal Lord and Savior with 100% assurance. This assurance is our goal!

> ### John 10:10
> [10]*The thief comes only to steal and kill and destroy...*

Trying to battle the enemy in a dark spiritual environment is dangerous. Battling Satan's game plan of "steal, kill and destroy" armed with only a 75%/25% victory/defeat ratio of assurance running through our friend's mind is a recipe for disaster! A 100% assurance is imperative. As heirs of the Kingdom, we are "more than conquerors"! Frequently, we are able to get these people back into church with us. Do not forget to pray for the job issues!

A 100% Meter Reading

Lastly, those in the 100% category are generally the happiest people on the face of the earth. They have found "peace, hope, joy and comfort that passes all understanding."

No matter what type of carnage life has thrown at them, they are walking with God. They are claiming the victory each day. I will ask them to share the 2-minute version of their salvation story with me. They love to share this because it takes them back to the roots of their spiritual rebirth. I enquire as to their church home and encourage them to be active. If they have drifted away from the church for whatever reason, I invite them to worship with me. As God's Forever Family, we need to be part of an active body of Christ. I will usually share my resources with them and challenge them to be a witnessing Christian.

Step 3 — The Give 'em Jesus Scriptures

Now we have reached Step 3. This step is the most important. Everything up to this point has been a strategic plan to get to the Give 'em Jesus Scriptures. The Scriptures are where the power is!

> ***Romans 1:16***
> *[16]For I am not ashamed of **the gospel**, for it **is the power of God for salvation to everyone who believes**, to the Jew first and also to the Greek.*

> ***1 Corinthians 1:18***
> *[18]For **the word of the cross** is folly to those who are perishing, but to us who are being saved it **is the power of God**.*

The Scriptures that you choose to use are totally up to your discretion. I have laid out five that I usually use for a 4-minute engagement in Appendix 1, page 138. Use those that have spoken to your heart over the years. You will automatically memorize these as you share them over and over. I had convinced myself that I could not memorize Scripture before I became a witness for Jesus. But, after only a few days, I had memorized all of my Give 'em Jesus Scriptures as those I witnessed to read them out loud over and over. It was automatic! Memorization is critical for another reason. As they read the verses, you will find yourself looking at their Testament or Scripture source upside down. Memorization is critically important!

Here is an effective method to apply the Scriptures.

Illustration: Pointing to the verse, ask:

"Would you read here, please?" (Pointing to the Scripture. While they read, we pray!)

"For God so loved the world ... " (John 3:16)

"What does this say to you?"

"God loves me."

"OK, would you read here, please?" (Pointing to the next Scripture. Praying!)

"For all have sinned ... " (Romans 3:23)

"What does this say to you?"

Continue right down the page or the Scripture source of your choice.

As strongly as I know how, I want to encourage you to have your Scriptures readily available in whatever format you choose. You can use a Bible, a telephone app, a quality tract, a Testament or this Handbook. **Whatever you decide to use, keep the verses at arm's length. Always!** In your pocket or in your purse, on your telephone, at the doors of your home, in your car, in your work vehicle or on your desk at all times so that no matter when or where the opportunity arises, you are ready by default. I have a buddy who stuffs them in his socks. He gives out around 1,500 Testaments each year. He enjoys watching many lost sinners make decisions for Christ.

I prefer the Testaments available from The Gideons International website through a free membership category called "Friends of the Gideons." With this free membership, the Testaments can be purchased for $2 (at the time of this publication). I prefer these for several reasons. First, it is my gift for those I witness to.

Second, the Scriptures are strategically laid out inside the back cover, easy to locate and ready to place into the nonbeliever's hands. I want them to touch the Word of God. I find this process to be much more effective, with them frequently holding the Word of God in their hands for the first time in their life! Think about it. At this point, they are holding the Word of God in their hands, reading with their eyes, from their lips, into their ears, through their mind and, hopefully, settling into their heart. Sometimes, I believe the Word of God seeps through their skin by osmosis! And, as a bonus, there may be second-hand listeners. Occasionally, I witness them make decisions for Jesus, too!

Third, if they make that decision for Jesus, there is a prayer of repentance and confession of faith paragraph. Just below is a place to record their name and date, which serves as a spiritual birth certificate and a future reminder of this very important day in their lives.

And fourth, the Testament is complete with the books of Psalms and Proverbs. For me, this is the perfect witnessing tool. If you prefer, you can have them read from this Handbook. Use what works best for you; however, I would urge consistency.

Step 4 — The Moment of Decision

Jesus told His disciples they would do even greater works than He. (John 14:12)

The greatest miracle in the world is when that lost sinner is spiritually "born again" and gets their name recorded in the Lamb's Book of Life. We must ensure we are prepared to experience this highest privilege. Sometimes it is not just one life that is made whole. It might be a family, a generation, a neighborhood, and, yes, perhaps even a nation!

Having clearly demonstrated the depravity of the human soul from sin and separation from God, it is now time for our friend to make a decision. What a travesty it would be to show someone the love of God but withhold the opportunity to receive it!

At this point, it is time to do a simple Gospel review to confirm their understanding of the Give 'em Jesus Scriptures you have now applied in Step 3. I predicate one question for each verse. You can apply your own questions for review based on the Give 'em Jesus Scriptures you choose for your application. The 5 Gospel Review Questions can be found in Appendix 1, Page 139.

Illustration: (Pointing to John 3:16, in my application) "Do you understand that God loves you?"

"Yes."

(Pointing to your next verse, in my application Romans 3:23) "Do you understand that you are a sinner in need of forgiveness?"

"Yes."

(Pointing to your next verse, in my application Romans 6:23) "Do you understand that Jesus died for full payment of your sins so you will have eternal life in Heaven?"

"Yes."

(Pointing to your next verse, in my application Rev. 3:20) "Do you understand that God is knocking at the door of your heart?"

"Yes."

(Pointing to your next verse, in my application John 1:12) "God promises salvation and eternal life in Heaven to every person who professes faith in Jesus, 100% guaranteed. Are you ready to invite Jesus into your heart?"

Total Silence — It's time to PRAY!

It is critically important for us to understand the spiritual dynamics at work in our friend's heart. The throne room of Heaven is rooting for you! The Word of God is applying pressure. We need to sit in stark silence and pray. Ten seconds for someone under conviction of the Holy Spirit seems like 10 hours! We have appropriately applied the Scriptures. The battle is now with God and His Word.

This moment is the pinnacle of spiritual warfare! Pray that Satan is bound but do not open your mouth until our lost friend breaks their silence.

When you ask Question 5, there are only two possible answers: "Yes" or "No."

If the answer is "Yes" and comes from the heart, at this definitive moment, there is a recording of their name in the Lamb's Book of Life! They are now officially "born again"! It is not when they recite The Sinner's Prayer, walk down an aisle or perform some ritual. The precise moment they place their faith and trust in the shed blood of Jesus Christ for the forgiveness of their sins, they receive their salvation! Oh, of course, we will lead them in The Sinner's Prayer or take their confession, (Appendix 1, pages 139, 140), whichever you prefer. The Bible substantiates both. Hearing them articulate their faith is just icing on the cake!

They will never forget this moment. When you tell a man about Jesus, he will never, ever forget. **Never!** They are now riding a spiritual rocket ship, angels are singing and your heart is rejoicing in God's goodness and the power of His Word!

Lastly, as a confirmation, I will apply the New Believer Questions found in Appendix 1, page 140. I will use these as time permits. Because this is designed to be a 4-minute presentation, time may be critical. If so, rather than the New Believer Questions, I may simply reapply the Acid Question for final assurance.

Illustration: "**NOW**, on a scale of 0%-100%, how certain are you that if you die today, you would spend eternity in Heaven?"

"**100%!**"

"Are you willing to claim this victory every day for the rest of your life?"

"Yes!"

The answer has to be an emphatic "100%." At this point, if my friend does not meter at 100%, I go back to the top of the Give 'em Jesus Scriptures and have them read again! (No matter how much time it takes. No matter how many times they have to read.) I do not leave this individual without a 100% assurance, ever!

But, what if the answer is "No"? What went wrong? Nothing went wrong. You were obedient to God, and you applied the Scriptures properly. Perhaps, there was no presence of the Holy Spirit even though they metered positive. Psychologists tell us the average person has to hear the message of the cross 7.6 times before they make that decision for Jesus. Maybe, we were #1 or #6. But, critically important is the fact we were obedient to God and perpetuated the cycle. Nothing confrontational! We always want to leave the ground fertile for the next witness for Jesus.

When I ask:

"Are you ready to invite Jesus Christ into your life and into your heart?" and I get a "No" response, I will gently apply the "Why" Principle (Appendix 1, page 140) twice. (Remember, they did test Holy Spirit positive!)

Illustration: "Are you ready to invite Jesus into your heart?"

"No."

"Why?"

"Not today."

"Why?"

"I have plenty of time." (Or, I am not ready now, etc.)

At this point, I may try to apply some Scriptures found in Chapter 4, Overcoming Objections.

"Look at this. (Page 78) The Word of God says in 2 Corinthians 6:2 'Today is the day of salvation. Now is the accepted time.' Tomorrow may never come! Proverbs 27:1 says, 'Do not count on tomorrow. We can't even predict what today might bring!' Would you be willing to reconsider and experience, right now, the peace and hope that comes with a 100% assurance of knowing the eternal destiny of your soul?"

I'm waiting for an answer. This is my last appeal!

If there is still no confirmation, I will ask my friend to read 1 John and if they will allow me to call them in a few days to see if the Scriptures have taken on any new meaning.

You may be wondering, is there some metric whereby I can gauge my soul-winning effectiveness? Well, yes, there is. It is called The Evaluation Gauge. So, how does it work, and what is the standard?

If 7.6 times is an accurate gauge for the number of times the average person must hear the message of the cross before giving their heart to Jesus, what does this imply? The implication is, if we live in an average world, talking to average people, under average circumstances and, assuming we are properly prepared — theoretically, it would be reasonable to expect to witness a decision for Jesus 1 out of every 7.6 times we share our faith. The question is, "Is this a reasonable assumption to measure our effectiveness?"

Let's go one step further: 1 as a percentage of 7.6 is 13%. What I have experienced over the years is this, no matter where I go: Times Square or Small Town, USA; "The Strip" in Las

Vegas or the neighborhood park; a controversial protest or a Christmas parade; an eventful demonstration or a flea market; a bus station or a bus stop; or anywhere else — at the end of the day, when I look at the decisions in my prayer book and count the number of times I shared my faith, the number of decisions is always around 13%, with one variant. When I go into dark spiritual environments; jails, prisons or places where worldly lusts allure, the percentages always go up. Sometimes significantly, 15%-18%! The Evaluation Gauge with a standard of 13% has proven to be a valuable assessment tool for me.

Remember, this is not a debate, a tug of war or an argument; by all means, do not let it end in that manner! **No matter what the decision is, you have been obedient to God. YOU HAVE BEEN SUCCESSFUL! Success is not measured in how much fruit you harvest. Success is measured in how much seed you sow. He is Lord of the harvest. He keeps the books. Always!!**

God wants to use you. When you are ready, God will use you. You may be amazed at what God chooses to do thru you! Apply the Spiritual Thermometer. Test every opportunity that comes your way. Search out where the Spirit of God is moving. Wherever you find the presence of the Holy Spirit, jump on board. You are never closer to God than when you tell that lost sinner about Jesus!

CHAPTER 2

CHAPTER 3

"FACE TO FACE" WITH DEATH! THE 10-SECOND OPPORTUNITY

We talked about the 30-minute presentation. We talked about the 4-minute presentation. But, what about the 10-second witness opportunity?

Some years ago, on a late Saturday afternoon, I was standing beside my truck in the barn yard when I heard what sounded like a high-speed vehicle collision just down the road. I, immediately, got in my truck and moments later found a small truck upside down in the road directly in front of my office door. After calling 911, I found two men. One was lying on the edge of the asphalt in a puddle of steaming hot oil and antifreeze. Chest crushed. Ribs broken.

To a man fighting for another breath of life:

"Are you willing to invite Jesus into your heart?"

"Are you willing to trust in His shed blood for the forgiveness of your sins?"

10 seconds!

If there is audible consent (a groan), visual consent (a muscle contraction), even undetectable mental consent or any other form of consent that comes, sincerely, from the heart, this man is saved!

Am I sure? Well, let's think about it for a moment. On the first Good Friday, three men were hanging on a cross. Two men were guilty. One man was innocent. The two who were guilty scoffed at Jesus. "If you really are the Son of God, save us all!" Moments later, one thief, in his heart, repented and rebuked the other thief, "Do you not fear God? We are guilty but this man is innocent!" He, then, looked at Jesus and said, "**Remember me** when you come into your Kingdom." Jesus said, "Today you will be with me in paradise!" (Mark 15:32, Luke 23:39-43)

No baptism. No communion. No sinner's prayer. No Bible. No Testament. No confirmation. No ritual. No church service. No kneeling. No hands lifted in worship. No "Just as I Am." No theologians. No evangelists. No church clothes. No mission trip. No cash. No credit card. He never volunteered. He never witnessed but to one man and he died lost in his sin hours later. Just a dying man on a cross who simply said, "**Remember me** when you come into your Kingdom!" He had nothing to offer except the confession of his sin and faith that Jesus was who He said He was!

That's it! And, yet, a career criminal walked into Heaven with Jesus, perhaps the same hour, as a child of God!

Sometimes, I believe, we overthink our responsibility of witnessing for Christ. At the root of it all, "Are you willing to invite Jesus into your heart? Are you willing to trust in His shed blood for the forgiveness of your sins?"

> ### *1 Peter 3:15*
> *[15]but in your hearts honor Christ the Lord as holy, **always being prepared** to make a defense to anyone who asks you for a reason for the hope that is in you; yet do it with gentleness and respect.*

So, whether your opportunity to share Christ is 30 minutes, 4 minutes or 10 seconds, you now have in your personal witnessing toolbox, a skill set that will fit every opportunity God provides. He wants you to experience this joy!

CHAPTER 3

CHAPTER 4

OVERCOMING OBJECTIONS

In the process of sharing our faith, we will encounter many objections. Sometimes the most challenging part of dealing with objections is unscrambling the real issue. Simply applying the "Why Principle" is the most effective way to get to the root. Once we know what these issues are, we can deal with them effectively.

You will find one source of help located in the very front of the Testament. "God's Help in Crisis" and "Help With Life's Problems" are simple reference guides to help in addressing these issues with Scripture. To effectively address these issues, we must be prepared to use the Word of God constantly, intelligently and convincingly.

To further assist, I am including a list of the most common objections encountered in dealing with those who are spiritually lost. Along with the objection, you will find a group of Scripture verses addressing the issue. I am listing familiar phrases from these verses to help you quickly identify the relevant texts you may choose to apply.

1. I MUST GET MY LIFE IN ORDER FIRST

Two men went up into
the temple.......................................Luke 18:10-14
Come not to call righteous but ....Matt. 9:13
I will arise and go to my father.......Luke 15:18-24
Look to me ....Isa. 45:22
You must make first things first.
Christ said, "Seek first the kingdom
of God."...Matt. 6:33
The story of the lost sheep..................Luke 15:1-7

**Christ alone can save you.
Come just as you are.**

2. I CANNOT FORGIVE

If you do not forgive others
their trespasses......................................Matt. 6:15
Be kind one to another ... forgiving.......Eph. 4:32
Forgive ... if you do not forgive .....Mark 11:25, 26
I can do all things through Christ..........Phil. 4:13
If anyone says, "I love God,"
and hates his brother...........................1 John 4:20

**Get to the Give 'em Jesus Scriptures
as soon as possible!**

3. I DON'T KNOW HOW TO BELIEVE

Believing means RECEIVING — HIM!

Whoever hears my word
and believes...John 5:24
For this is the will of my Father........ John 6:40-47
Whoever believes in
him should not.......................................John 3:16

To all who did receive

him, ... he gave ....John 1:12

He will come and save you...................Isa. 35:3, 4

With the heart one believes ....Rom. 10:9, 10

I. Repent ....Acts 2:38; 3:19

II. Be Converted......................Matt. 13:15; 18:3

III. Believe and Be

Born Again ....John 3:3; 1:12

    Believe what God says is TRUE.

4. I AM A CHURCH MEMBER

You are depending upon your profession.

Strive for peace ... holiness

without which..Heb. 12:14

They profess to know God, but .... Titus 1:16

If someone says he has faith, but........ James 2:14

Unless one is born again he cannot ....John 3:3

By grace you have been saved

through faith........................ Eph. 2:8, 9; Gal. 2:16;

Rom 11:6; 2 Tim. 1:9; Matt. 15:7, 8; 7:21-23; 6:24;

Matt. 18:3; Luke 14:11; Matt.10:32

You Must Be Born Into God's Family.

Looking to Jesus, the founder and perfecter
of our faith, who for the joy that was set
before him endured the cross, despising
the shame, and is seated at the right hand of
the throne of God............................ Hebrews 12:2

5. IT MAKES NO DIFFERENCE WHAT I BELIEVE AS LONG AS I AM SINCERE

Believing means RECEIVING — HIM!

Christ said it makes all the

difference in the world ....Mark 16:16

May be sincerely wrong.......................Prov. 16:25

I am the way................................John 14:6; 20:31

I am the resurrection ....John 11:25

He that believes.......................................Rom. 4:5

All may be condemned who
did not believe the truth............... 2 Thes. 2:10-12

Believe in
Him.........John 3:3, 18, 36; 5:24; 12:48; Acts 13:39;
                    Rom. 10:4, 10; 2 Cor. 5:17; 1 John 5:13

**Get to the Give 'em Jesus Scriptures
as soon as possible!**

6. GOD IS TOO GOOD TO DAMN ANYONE

**God does NOT damn anyone. Man damns
himself when he refuses to believe in Christ.
Man closes the doors of Heaven in his own face.**

Whoever does not
believe ....Mark 16:16; John 3:18, 36

Yet you refuse to come to me
that you may ....John 5:40

I have no pleasure ... for why
will you die? ....Ezek. 33:11

If God did not spare angels .... 2 Peter 2:4, 6, 9

Unless you repent, you will
all ... perish .... Luke 13:3

There is no peace ... for the wicked ....Isa. 57:21

God's kindness is meant to
lead you..Rom. 2:4, 5

You would die in your sins ....John 8:21, 24

7. BACKSLIDERS

The backslider's life is a constant dishonor to himself.

Your evil will chastise you, and your
apostasy will reprove you .... Jer. 2:19

I will spit you out of my mouth .... Rev. 3:16

The last state has become worse
for them than the first .... 2 Pet. 2:20

Return, O faithless children .... Jer. 3:14

I will heal their apostasy .... Hosea 14:4

I acknowledged my sin ... and you
forgave .... Ps. 32:5

If we confess our sins, he is faithful ...... 1 John 1:9

If anyone does sin, we have
an advocate .... 1 John 2:1

If my people ... turn from their ...... 2 Chron. 7:14;
Jer. 2:5, 13; Amos 4:11, 12; Jer. 3:12, 13, 22; Isa.
44:22-25; Deut. 4:28-31; 2 Chron. 15:4; 33:12, 13;
Luke 15:13-24

Joy, power for service await a
returning backslider .... Ps. 51:12, 13

8. I WILL NOT BE ACCEPTED

Christ Jesus came ... to
save sinners .... 1 Tim. 1:15

While we were still sinners .... Rom. 5:8

Though your sins are like scarlet .... Isa. 1:18

The Son of Man came to seek
and to save .... Luke 19:10

The Spirit and the Bride
say, "Come." .... Rev. 22:17

I came not to call the righteous ....Matt. 9:13

I, I am he who blots out ....Isa. 43:25

I have no pleasure in the
death of the wicked...............................Ezek. 33:11

I have blotted out ....Isa. 44:22

As far as the east is from the west ....Ps. 103:12

Everyone who calls ....Rom. 10:13

God was moved by his entreaty....2 Chron. 33:13

**Get to the Give 'em Jesus Scriptures
as soon as possible!**

9. FRIENDS WILL HARASS ME

All who desire to live a godly life in
Christ Jesus will be persecuted............2 Tim. 3:12

If we endure, we will also reign............2 Tim. 2:12

Sufferings of this present time are
not worth comparing ....Rom. 8:18

For what does it profit a man ....Mark 8:36

For whoever is ashamed of me..............Mark 8:38

Rejoicing that they were counted
worthy to suffer ....Acts 5:41

For to this you have been called .....1 Pet. 2:20, 21

The fear of man lays a snare ....Prov. 29:25

Friendship with the world is
enmity with God .... James 4:4

Blessed is the man who walks
not in the counsel.....................................Ps. 1:1, 2

Our fellowship is with the Father ....1 John 1:3

If you were of the world ....John 15:18, 19

Blessed are you when others
revile you and persecute you ....Matt. 5:11, 12

Through many tribulations .... Acts 14:22
Endured the cross,
despising the shame ....Heb. 12:2, 3
But seek first the kingdom of God ....Matt. 6:33

**Get to the Give'em Jesus Scriptures
as soon as possible!**

10. I AM DOING THE BEST I CAN

**The "Best you can" is to repent, receive Christ
and serve Him.**

Unless you repent, you
will ... perish .... Luke 13:3, 5
Not to call the righteous, but sinners ...Mark 2:17
God's kindness is meant to lead
you to repentance ....Rom. 2:4
The whole world may be held
accountable to God........................... Rom. 3:19-24
A person is not justified by works
of the law but through faith.....................Gal. 2:16
Unless your righteousness exceeds......Matt. 5:20
All who rely on works of the law
are under a curse.......................................Gal. 3:10
Whoever keeps the whole law but
fails in one point................................... James 2:10
You shall love the Lord your God with all your
heart and with all your soul and with all your
mind. This is the great and first commandment.
Matt. 22:37, 38

11. I DO NOT BELIEVE THE BIBLE

If anyone's will is to do
God's will..John 7:17; 12:46

For the word of the cross ....1 Cor. 1:18
Even if our gospel is veiled .... 2 Cor. 4:3-6
You will die in your sin......................John 8:21-24
You who are afflicted ....2 Thes. 1:7, 8
Whoever believes and is baptized......Mark 16:16
The natural person does not accept....1 Cor. 2:14
The friendship of the Lord is for those
who fear him..Ps. 25:14
For the wisdom of this world ....1 Cor. 3:19
Whoever believes in him is not ....John 3:18
He will convict the world
concerning sin......................................John 16:8, 9
Anyone who has set aside the
law of Moses ....Heb. 10:28, 29
And whosoever was not
found written...Rev. 20:15
How shall we escape...................................Heb. 2:3
Whoever believes in the Son..................John 3:36

**Get to the Give 'em Jesus Scriptures
as soon as possible!**

12. EARNEST-MINDED SKEPTICS

Natural person does not accept............1 Cor. 2:14
How unsearchable are
his judgments ....Rom. 11:33
When I was a child ... when I became a
man ... then I shall know fully...... 1 Cor. 13:11, 12
Put your finger here ....John 20:24-29
This is the judgment................................John 3:19
Written so that you may believe ....John 20:31
Saul's conversion.................................Acts 26:9-20
The friendship of the Lord
is for those..Ps. 25:14

If they do not hear Moses .... Luke 16:31
If we deny him, he also will
deny us .... 2 Tim. 2:12, 13
Everyone who looks on the Son and
believes in him .... John 6:40
If anyone's will is to do God's will,
he will know .... John 7:17
Making known to us the mystery
of his will .... Eph. 1:9-18
    Also: John 1:45-49; 2 Cor. 3:3, 4, 14-16.

13. TOO MUCH TO GIVE UP

Can you afford NOT to be a Christian?
For what does it profit a man .... Mark 8:36, 37

What you now have is worthless.
And the world is passing away .... 1 John 2:17
For the word of the cross .... 1 Cor. 1:18

Loss for Christ is real gain.
For the love of money is a root .... 1 Tim. 6:10
But whatever gain I had .... Phil. 3:7-9
But seek first the kingdom of God .... Matt. 6:33
But Abraham said, "Child,
remember ... " .... Luke 16:25

What it cost Christ to die for you.
But emptied himself .... Phil. 2:7, 8
No good thing does he withhold .... Ps. 84:11
We know that for those who love
God all things .... Rom. 8:28-32
He who loves money .... Ecc. 5:10
Friendship with the world
is enmity .... James 4:4

Do not love the world .... 1 John 2:15-17
For the one who sows to
his own flesh.. Gal. 6:8
For Christ has entered, not into.............Heb. 9:24

14. NOT NOW, I HAVE PLENTY OF TIME

Behold, now is the favorable time .... 2 Cor. 6:2
Choose this day whom you
will serve .... Josh. 24:15
How long will you go .... 1 Kings 18:21
Today, if you hear his voice .... Ps. 95:7-9
Do not boast about tomorrow .... Prov. 27:1
Remember also your Creator...................Ecc. 12:1
Come now, let us reason together...........Isa. 1:18
Seek the Lord while he may be
found ....Isa. 55:6
You also must be ready........................Matt. 24:44
Your soul is required
of you..................................... Luke 12:19, 20; 13:24
And now why do you wait? .... Acts 22:16
You do not know what
tomorrow ....James 4:13-14
As long as it is called "today," .... Heb. 3:13, 15
But seek first the
kingdom of God ....Matt. 6:33
My Spirit shall not abide
in man forever ....Gen. 6:3

Do it today! You are never promised another day nor hour—just one heartbeat between you and eternity. Delays are always

dangerous—God will eventually surrender you to the desires of your heart.

Get to the Give 'em Jesus Scriptures as soon as possible!

15. CHRISTIANS ARE HYPOCRITICAL

It is better to spend a short while with some of the hypocrites here on earth, rather than spend a long eternity with all of them in Hell! All hypocrites will perish.

Such are the paths of all............................ Job 8:13

Christ alone is the pattern.

Neither be called instructors .... Matt. 23:10

Turn to me and be saved .... Isa. 45:22

Judge not, that you be not judged ...... Matt. 7:1-5

So then each of us .... Rom. 14:12

Therefore you have no excuse............. Rom. 2:1-5

And it shall be like people .... Hosea 4:9

When Peter saw him, he said

to Jesus .... John 21:21, 22

Behold, all souls are mine .... Ezek. 18:4

Do not judge by appearances .... John 7:24

Being ignorant of the righteousness

of God... Rom. 10:3

It is not the one who

commends himself .... 2 Cor. 10:18

For it is time for judgement .... 1 Peter 4:17

And will cut him in pieces and put him with the hypocrites. In that place there will be weeping and gnashing of teeth. .... Matt. 24:51

Get to the Give 'em Jesus Scriptures as soon as possible!

16. I AM TOO GREAT A SINNER

Though your sins are like scarlet .... Isa. 1:18

Son of Man came to seek
and to save .... Luke 19:10

God, be merciful to me, a sinner! .... Luke 18:13

Christ died for the ungodly .... Rom. 5:6

Christ Jesus came ... to save sinners.... 1 Tim. 1:15

Made him to be sin for us, that we ...... 2 Cor. 5:21

He loved us and sent his Son .... 1 John 4:10

He is able to save to the uttermost .... Heb. 7:25

For I came not to call the
righteous, but sinners. .... Matt. 9:12, 13

Let the wicked forsake ... he may
have compassion ... he will abundantly
pardon .... Isa. 55:7

Turn to me and be saved .... Isa. 45:22

I am he who blots out
your transgressions .... Isa. 43:25

The Spirit and the Bride
say, "Come." .... Rev. 22:17

I have no pleasure in the death of the
wicked, why will you die .... Ezek. 33:11

**The very fact that you acknowledge your sin
is evidence that the Spirit has brought you
under conviction and that you are very near
the Kingdom. Christ is able to save YOU,
NOW, just as you are.**

He will convict the world
concerning sin .... John 16:8-11

If we walk in the light ... the blood
of Jesus his Son cleanses us .... 1 John 1:7

David was a great sinner .... Ps. 32
The woman at the well,
an adulteress .... John 4:1-42
Saul of Tarsus, a murderer .... 1 Tim. 1:13-15
Manasseh, all godlessness ...... 2 Chron. 33:12, 13
All that the Father gives me will come to me,
and whoever comes to me
I will never cast out .... John 6:37

17. I CAN EARN MY SALVATION

You must be born again.

Unless one is born again .... John 3:3-8
Therefore, if anyone is in Christ .... 2 Cor. 5:17
Everyone who practices righteousness
has been born of him .... 1 John 2:29
No chance after death .... 2 Cor. 5:10
After that comes judgment .... Heb. 9:27
Everyone who has been
born of God .... 1 John 5:4
He gave the right to become
children of God .... John 1:12
You have been born again,
not of perishable .... 1 Pet. 1:23

Salvation is never of works.

By grace you have been saved through faith ...
not a result of works, so that no
one may boast .... Eph. 2:8, 9
To the one who does not work
but believes .... Rom. 4:5
Not because of our works .... 2 Tim. 1:9

God's children have joy of assurance.

My sheep hear my voice ... and they will
never perish ....John 10:27-29

By him everyone who believes
is freed ....Acts 13:38, 39

Confess with your mouth that
Jesus is Lord and believe ...
you will be saved ....Rom. 10:9, 10

He is faithful and just to forgive ....1 John 1:9

One God ... one mediator ...
Christ Jesus ....1 Tim. 2:5

Search the Scriptures.............................John 5:39

Examining the Scriptures daily............ Acts 17:11

Like newborn infants, long for the
pure spiritual milk................................1 Pet. 2:1, 2

Are you trusting in Christ or the church?

No one can lay a foundation ....1 Cor. 3:11

There is salvation in no one else for
there is no other name.............................Acts 4:12

For the law...can never...
make perfect.. Heb. 10:1-3

Every priest stands daily at his service...
which can never take away sins.....Heb. 10:11, 12

We have confidence to enter the holy
places by the blood of Jesus ....Heb. 10:19, 20

18. HOW DO WE KNOW THERE IS A GOD

By creation.

God has shown it to them .... Rom. 1:19-22

The heavens declare glory of God ....Ps. 19:1

The fool says in his heart,
"There is no God." ....Ps. 14:1

By revelation (His Word, the Bible).

God spoke all these words ....Ex. 20:1

God spoke to our fathers ....Heb. 1:1

Through His Son, the Lord Jesus Christ.

He was manifested in the flesh............ 1 Tim. 3:16

He was in the form of God .... Phil. 2:6, 7

I am in the Father and the Father is in me...

I do not speak on my

own authority ....John 14:10, 11

The glory that I had with you ....John 17:5

He was rich...he became poor ....2 Cor. 8:9

By Godly men.

For I am not ashamed (Paul) ....Rom. 1:16

19. I HAVE NOT FINISHED "SOWING WILD OATS"

For the wages of sin is death ....Rom. 6:23

Then desire when it has conceived .... James 1:15

Do not boast about tomorrow .... Prov. 27:1

God will bring you into judgment ....Ecc. 11:9

Whatever one sows ....Gal. 6:7

Friendship with the world is enmity

with God .... James 4:4

For to set the mind on the flesh............. Rom. 8:6

20. UNPARDONABLE SIN

Therefore I tell you, every sin and blasphemy will be forgiven people, but the blasphemy against the Spirit will not be forgiven........Matt. 12:31, 32

This describes those who, knowing the work is the work of the Holy Spirit deliberately describe it as the work of Satan.

21. I DO NOT HAVE TO ACCEPT CHRIST OPENLY

Christ says you do have to confess me openly!

Everyone who acknowledges
me before men ....Matt. 10:32
Confess with your mouth **(openly)** .....Rom. 10:9
With the mouth one
confesses **(openly)** ....Rom. 10:10
Everyone who calls upon the name ....Acts 2:21
Do not be ashamed of the testimony... 2 Tim. 1:8
Whoever is ashamed of me ....Mark 8:38
Whoever confesses that Jesus ....1 John 4:15
Open my lips...Ps. 51:15

He died OPENLY for you; you must confess Him OPENLY!

22. I FEEL SAVED

Depending on feeling is not faith.

Without faith it is impossible ....Heb. 11:6
Whoever believes in the Son..................John 3:36
Pharisee and tax collector ....Luke 18:9-14
There is a way that seems right .... Prov. 14:12
In hope of eternal life............................. Titus 1:2
The heart is deceitful above all .... Jer. 17:9

It is not what we FEEL, but what GOD SAYS!

Many FEEL saved depending on feeling — it is not a feeling that saves, but the fact of the new birth.

23. THIS WORLD HAS MUCH MORE TO OFFER

Do not love the world .... 1 John 2:15-17
You adulterous people! ... friendship
with the world is enmity with God .... James 4:4
You cannot drink the cup .... 1 Cor. 10:21
Riches choke the word .... Matt. 13:22
Whoever loves pleasure will be
a poor man .... Prov. 21:17
Who is self-indulgent is dead .... 1 Tim. 5:6
Cannot be my disciple ..... Luke 14:33; Heb. 11:24
(Moses); Phil. 3:7 (Paul)
So, whether you eat or drink .... 1 Cor. 10:31
The trouble is the pleasures of this world are not innocent. They choke the Gospel, hindering salvation and service.

24. WHAT ABOUT THE HEATHEN WHO HAD NO CHANCE?

The Bible says they are without excuse.
Wrath of God is revealed from
heaven against all ungodliness .... Rom. 1:18
God has shown it to them .... Rom. 1:18-32
Wrath of God is revealed .... Rom. 1:18-24
Result of Gentile
World apostasy .... Rom. 1:24-32
Pagan moralizers bad
as other pagans .... Rom. 2:1-16

All the heathens are lost.
The Father judges no one, but has
given all judgment to the Son ....John 5:22
Truly, truly, I say to you ....John 5:25
And he has given him authority ....John 5:27

25. I CAN'T GIVE UP MY COMPANIONS

They'll give YOU up if YOU are really born again.
The companion of fools will
suffer harm .... Prov. 13:20
Blessed is the man who walks not............Psa. 1:1
Our fellowship is with the Father ....1 John 1:3
Friendship with the world is
enmity with God .... James 4:4
My son, if sinners entice you............Prov. 1:10-15
Be not envious of evil men,
nor desire to be with them .... Prov. 24:1, 2
One who is full loathes honey............... Prov. 27:7
Bad company ruins good morals ......1 Cor. 15:33
The fear of man lays a snare .... Prov. 29:25

**Get to the Give 'em Jesus Scriptures
as soon as possible!**

26. I DON'T HAVE TO GO TO CHURCH

**But you will want to! It is only natural for the
child of God to be in the house of God, his
Father.**
Not neglecting to meet together ....Heb. 10:25
They devoted themselves to the apostles'
teaching and the fellowship....................Acts 2:42
All who believed were together ....Acts 2:44

And day by day, attending
the temple ....Acts 2:46
You too may have fellowship
with us ....1 John 1:3
**True, one does not have to go to church to
be a Christian. One does need the fellowship
the church provides, especially since we
mingle with the world during the week.
You need the church. The church needs
you. Where are they looking for you? "Birds
of a feather flock together." They found Christ
in the temple. Luke 2:42-49.**

27. I WAS ALWAYS A CHRISTIAN

If you were, Christ would not have told you:
Unless one is born again ....John 3:3
Behold, I was brought forth in iniquity, and
in sin did my mother conceive me ....Ps. 51:5
For all have sinned and fall short
of the glory of God..................................Rom. 3:23
We have all become like one who is unclean,
and all our righteous deeds are like a
polluted garment ....Isa. 64:6
The heart is deceitful above
all things... Jer. 17:9, 10
All we like sheep have gone astray ....Isa. 53:6
There is not a righteous
man on earth ....Ecc. 7:20
But God shows his love for us in that while
we were still sinners,
Christ died for us......................................Rom. 5:8
But to all who did receive him, who believed

87

in his name he gave the right to become
children of God ....John 1:12
**If you were always a Christian you would not
have to become one as Christ here strictly says.**

28. I CANNOT UNDERSTAND THE BIBLE

**Of course you cannot understand. No
unregenerate person can. God gives the
reason for it in His book, the Bible.**

The natural person does
not accept .... 1 Cor. 2:14
It is veiled to those who
are perishing.. 2 Cor. 4:3, 4
Their minds were hardened .... 2 Cor. 3:14, 16
Some things are hard to
understand ....2 Pet. 3:16-18
My thoughts are not your thoughts..... Isa. 55:8, 9
The one who...does not receive
my words...John 12:48
Open my eyes ....Psa. 119:18
I understood as a child .... 1 Cor. 13:11, 12
How unsearchable
are his judgments...................................Rom. 11:33
For no prophecy was
ever produced .... 2 Pet. 1:21
If anyone's will is to do God's will, he will know
whether the teaching is from God or whether
I am speaking on my own authority......John 7:17

29. I AM TRYING TO BE A CHRISTIAN

**Trusting, NOT trying, saves. Trusting Christ
and His finished work on the cross saves us.**

Believe in the Lord Jesus .... Acts 16:31

Whoever believes has ....John 6:47

Work of God, that you believe in him .....John 6:29

By grace you have been saved .... Eph 2:8, 9

Not by trying, but by faith.

Now faith is the assurance of things......Heb. 11:1

Faith working through love ....Gal. 5:6

You must be born from above (again) before you can carry the family name of Christ. You cannot join a family to become their child, but must be born into it. Then, and only then, have you the right, the authority from God, to call yourself a Son of God.

John 1:11, 12 Also: 1 John 5:4, 5, make
this very clear. It is a birth, not a joining.
Rom. 3:23-25; 4:3-5; 2 Tim. 1:12.

I will trust, and will not be afraid ....Isa. 12:2

Who by God's power are being guarded
through faith...1 Pet. 1:5

30. I HAVE TRIED ONCE BUT FAILED

I cannot hold out. You are not asked to hold out.

The Lord upholds his hand .... Ps. 37:23, 24

Him who is able to keep you
from stumbling..Jude 24

He is able to guard .... 2 Tim. 1:12

Christ who lives in me ....Gal. 2:20

He who began a good work......................Phil. 1:6

He is able to save to the uttermost ....Heb. 7:25

They will never perish..................... John 10:27-29

Who by God's power are
being guarded ....1 Pet. 1:5; 4:19
God is faithful, and he will not let you be tempted
beyond your ability, but with the temptation he
will also provide the way of escape.....1 Cor. 10:13
I will heal their apostasy.......................Hosea 14:4
Son of Man came to
seek and to save....................................Luke 19:10
God is able to make all
grace abound...2 Cor. 9:8
**If you have made a full surrender to God, you
will not fail. Many fail because they do not
confess Christ in their lives.**

31. I AM NOT A SINNER; I AM GOOD ENOUGH

If we say we have not sinned we make Him a liar.
If we say we have not sinned...............1 John 1:10
If I had cherished iniquity in
my heart..Ps. 66:18
Love the Lord your God with all
your heart..Matt. 22:37
For by works of the law ....Rom. 3:20-23
For the wages of sin is death ....Rom. 6:23
As it is written: "None is righteous,
no, not one;" ....Rom. 3:10
Whoever believes in him is
not condemned..John 3:18
Now we know that whatever
the law says ....Rom. 3:19, 20
To you who are afflicted .... 2 Thes. 1:7-9
For by grace you have been saved .... Eph. 2:8, 9
Not by works of righteousness................ Titus 3:5
Without faith it is impossible ......Heb. 11:6; 10:28

Let it be known to
you therefore ....Acts 13:38, 39
A person is not justified............ Gal. 2:16, 21; 3:10
You would die in your sins, for
unless you ....John 8:24, 34
And to the one who does not work ....Rom. 4:5
What must we do, to be doing the works
of God? ....John 6:28
Surely there is not a righteous man........Ecc. 7:20
All we like sheep have gone astray ....Isa. 53:6
We have all become like one
who is unclean ....Isa. 64:6

**Get to the Give 'em Jesus Scriptures
as soon as possible!**

32. THE BIBLE IS NOT GOD'S WORD

We know that the Bible is the Word of God
because of its own claim to inspiration.
Expressions like "The Lord said," "The Lord
Spoke," "The Word of the Lord Came," "Thus
says the Lord," occur over 3,000times in the Bible.

**All men who wrote the Bible were inspired
by God.**

Moses and Aaron .... Exodus 4:15
King David .... 2 Sam. 23:2; Acts 1:16
Prophet Ezekiel ....Ezek. 12:21
Paul, the apostle to the
Gentiles ....2 Tim. 3:16, 17; 1 Thess. 2:13
Peter, the apostle to the Jews................ 2 Pet. 1:21

**The testimony of Christ Himself proves the
divine authority of the Old Testament
Scriptures.**

And beginning at Moses and
all the prophets............................... Luke 24:27, 44
Here Jesus brings in the three divisions of the
Old Testament, accepting them all as being the
Word of God.

The New Testament:
But the Helper .... John 14:26
Heaven and earth will pass away .... Matt. 24:35
For truly, I say to you.............................. Matt. 5:18
If he called them gods.......................... John 10:35
And beginning with Moses .... Luke 24:27-44
And we also thank God
constantly for this............................... 1 Thess. 2:13
We have the prophetic word
more fully... 2 Pet. 1:19-21;
1 John 5:10; John 8:47

33. CHRIST IS COMING AGAIN SOON

How did Christ come the first time?
Born of woman... Gal. 4:4
Conceived of the Holy Spirit .... Matt. 1:18-23
And the Word became flesh................... John 1:14
Born in the likeness of men .... Phil. 2:6-8

What He said about His going away.
I am going to him who sent me .... John 7:33
Glorify me in your own presence .... John 17:5

Did He return to Heaven never again to return to earth? Here are His own words.
For the Son of Man is going to come with
his angels in the glory of his Father .... Matt. 16:27
Also: Matt. 23:39; 24:3-7, 27-31, 36-51; 25:3-13;

26:63, 64; Mark 8:38; 13:24-27, 32-37; 14:61, 62;
Luke 9:26; 12:35-46; 13:34, 35; 17:20-37; 18:8;
19:11-27; 21:25-36; John 14:1-3, 28; 21:2-24.

When He comes again, He will be SEEN with our bodily eyes.

This Jesus, who was taken up from you into
heaven, will come in the same way as you
saw him go into heaven .... Acts 1:9-11
Also: Matt. 24:27; Luke 17:24; Phil. 3:20, 21;
1 Thess. 4:16, 17; 2 Thess. 1:7-10; 1 John 3:2;
Rev. 1:7.

His second coming will be physical and outward.

For this we declare to you .... 1 Thess. 4:15
and said, "Men of Galilee ..." .... Acts 1:11
Behold, he is coming with the clouds ...... Rev. 1:7
And when he had said
these things .... Acts 1:9-11

34. HEAVEN

Heaven is a prepared place for prepared people.

In my Father's house are
many rooms .... John 14:2, 3
A house not made with
 hands, eternal .... 2 Cor. 5:1
No eye has seen, nor ear heard .... 1 Cor. 2:9
He has prepared for them a city .... Heb. 11:16
Here we have no lasting city .... Heb. 13:14
Looking forward to the city that
has foundations .... Heb. 11:10
Lay up for yourselves treasures
in heaven .... Matt. 6:20

**Heaven: A place of wonderful description —
Marvelously built.** And He carried me away
in the Spirit to a great and high mountain, and
showed me that great city, the Holy Jerusalem,
descending out of heaven from God....Rev. 21:10

Gloriously lighted. And the city had no need
of the sun, neither of the moon, to shine in
it; for the glory of God did lighten it, and the
Lamb is the light thereof. Rev.21:23

Righteously governed. And there shall be no
more curse: but the throne of God and of the
Lamb shall be in it; and His servants shall
serve Him. ....Rev. 22:3

**A place of absolute perfection and
perfect purity**...Rev. 21:27

35. HELL
Christ says there is a Hell.

The wicked shall be turned into hell .... Ps. 9:17

And if your hand causes you to sin .... Mark 9:43

Fear him who, after he has killed,
has authority to cast into hell .... Luke 12:5

Where is Hell? At the end of a godless life.

The path of life leads upward for the prudent,
that he may turn away from
Sheol beneath .... Prov. 15:24

You will be brought
down to Hades .... Matt. 11:23

Hell is away from God.

Depart from me, you cursed, into
the eternal fire .... Matt. 25:41-46

Hell is where Heaven is not.
Abraham speaks to the rich man in Hell and says:

And besides all this, between us and you a great
chasm has been fixed .... Luke 16:26

The Bible plainly teaches that Hell is somewhere: beneath, down, away from God, where Heaven is not.

The Way to Hell.

For the gate is wide and the way is easy
that leads to destruction, and those who
enter by it are many .... Matt. 7:13

It is easily found: The gate is wide. Not difficult to keep in it. Broad is the way. It is

jammed with travelers. Those who enter by it are many.

And cast the worthless servant
into the outer darkness.........................Matt. 25:30

For whom the gloom of utter darkness has
been reserved forever. ....Jude 13

Other verses to use: Rev. 14:10; 21:8;
2 Pet. 2:4-13.

**Hell was not made for man, but for the
devil and his angels** ....Matt. 25:41

36. MORE SALVATION VERSES

You need to be saved!
Unless one is born again ....John 3:3
All have sinned and fall short ......Rom. 3:23; 6:23
There is not a righteous
man on earth ....Ecc. 7:20
All we like sheep have gone astray ....Isa. 53:6
We have all become like one
who is unclean ....Isa. 64:6
The heart is deceitful above all ....Jer. 17:9, 10
Unless you repent ....Luke 13:3

You cannot save yourself.
For my thoughts are not
your thoughts ....Isa. 55:8
Not by works of righteousness................ Titus 3:5
For whoever keeps the whole law ...... James 2:10
By works of the law no one will be ....Gal. 2:16
There is a way that seems right ....Prov. 14:12
Jesus said to him, "I am the way ... " .....John 14:6
By works of the law no human will
be justified ....Rom. 3:20
For after that in the wisdom of God .... 1 Cor. 1:21

God has provided for your salvation.
God shows his love for us........................Rom. 5:8

He himself bore our sins .... 1 Pet. 2:24
Him to be sin who knew no sin .... 2 Cor. 5:21
All this is from God .... 2 Cor. 5:18, 19
For I delivered to you as of first........ 1 Cor. 15:3, 4
For by grace you have been saved
through faith.. Eph. 2:8, 9

Believe God's Word and be saved.
Jesus answered them ....John 6:29
Truly, truly, I say to you,
whoever hears ....John 5:24
Whoever has the Son has life .... 1 John 5:12
I write these things to you .... 1 John 5:13

Must confess Jesus before men.
Everyone who
acknowledges me...........................Matt. 10:32, 33
For whoever is ashamed of me............. Luke 9:26
If you confess with your...................Rom. 10:9, 10

Saving faith produces good works.
What good is it ...
if someone says ....James 2:14-18
For it is God who works in you .... Phil. 2:13
I want you to insist on these things .... Titus 3:8
Remember: Each of us will give
an account ....Rom. 14:12
It is appointed for man to die once ....Heb. 9:27
Choose this day whom
you will serve ....Jos. 24:15

37. MORE ASSURANCE VERSES

We may KNOW that our sins are forgiven.
These things have I written .... 1 John 5:13
To him all the prophets
bear witness................................ Acts 10:43, 13:39
Truly, truly, I say to you ....John 5:24
Whoever believes in the Son has...........John 3:36

**The Spirit himself bears witness with our
spirit that we are children of God (Rom. 8:16)**
What is meant by the witness of the Spirit? Is
it a feeling within us by which we know we are
the children of God? Certainly not! The Word
of God is the testimony of the Spirit. What
God has written in His Word concerning our
redemption, justification, security, etc., these
are the witness, or testimony of the Spirit, since
they are given by inspiration of the Spirit. The
evidence of ownership of a home is not the way
you feel, or the fact that you see it, but the deed
and what is written therein. The Word of God is
His deed. This never changes and never fails.

REFUTING FALSE DOCTRINE

In a broad-based culture such as ours, we will encounter many false beliefs and cults. Many will deny us the opportunity to open our Bibles. Many are not interested in anything but their own beliefs. But, we never allow ourselves to become confrontational. We never get into arguments or shouting matches, and we never engage in anything that would bring detriment to the cause of Christ. If someone will not take God at His Word, they will not take you at yours. The challenging task is trying to discern between those who are intentionally confrontational and those searching for truth. When we can understand the false doctrine behind these belief systems, it makes sharing the Gospel much easier and more effective.

Below is a list of some specific religions and cults we will encounter and a brief summary of their beliefs. Understanding their beliefs will give us a definitive edge as we share the life changing message of the Gospel with them! As we open the Scriptures to refute their false beliefs, those truly seeking truth are attentive. We will shift to the Give 'em Jesus Scriptures at the appropriate time and pursue a decision for Jesus!

A SAMPLING OF WESTERN RELIGIONS
Catholicism

Catholics believe that sacred performances of the seven sacraments are all a part of salvation.

- Baptism — Sprinkling, usually an infant, to wash away "original" sins.
- Eucharist — Lord's Supper. Believe that it becomes the literal body and blood of Christ.
- Reconciliation — Penance. The way you pay for your sins.
- Confirmation — The study and pledge of devotion and allegiance to "the church."
- Marriage — Must be married in "the church" or else not right before God.
- Holy Orders — Devotion and allegiance to the hierarchy of priests and the Pope.
- Anointing of the Sick — Last Rights. Final pledge to faith in "the church" for salvation.

See: Ephesians 2:8-9; Titus 3:5; 1 Peter 1:17-19

- Mariolatry

This is the belief that Mary is the "Mother of God," and that she possesses the grace to grant eternal salvation. She is the advocate and mediatrix of the blood of Christ. A rosary is an object used to pray to Mary for the salvation of the soul.

See: John 2:5; 1 Timothy 2:5; Hebrews 9:14, 15; 1 John 2:1

- Confession

This is the belief that one must confess their sins to a priest and receive absolution to obtain forgiveness. Without confession, you cannot keep your salvation.

See: Psalm 32:5; Matthew 23:8-10; 1 John 1:9

- Infant baptism

This is the practice of sprinkling infants with "holy water" to wash away "original sin" and make them part of "the church." These children will later go through their catechism and confirmation to reaffirm their devotion to "the church."

See: Acts 2:41; Acts 8:12; Acts 18:8

- Purgatory

This is the belief that there is a place of temporary punishment to purge the soul. Thus, everyone will eventually get to Heaven once they have paid the price for their sins. This dogma is from the Apocryphal book of 2 Maccabees 12.

See: Luke 16:22, 23; 1 John 1:7; Revelation 20:12-15; Revelation 21:27

Jehovah's Witness

- Total annihilation

This is the belief that when a person dies without being one of Jehovah's Witnesses, they pass into oblivion. They believe there is no punishment or afterlife for those who have rejected the "truth" they teach.

See: Mark 9:44-48; Revelation 14:10, 11;
Revelation 20:10

- Deny a literal burning Hell

This is the belief that Hell is figurative, not an actual, literal place of fire.

See: Matt. 10:28; Luke 16:22, 23;
Revelation 20:12-15; Revelation 21:8

- Deny the deity of Christ

Denial of Biblical fact that Jesus is God the Son is the greatest heresy possible.

See: Matthew 1:23; John 1:1-4, 14; John 20:28;
Philippians 2:10, 11; 2 John 1:9

- Deny the resurrection of Christ

Denial of Biblical fact the literal bodily resurrection of Jesus Christ is heresy. Jehovah's Witnesses like to spiritualize things in Scripture they disagree with as occurring in a spiritual context but not in reality. The Resurrection of Jesus Christ is one of those things.

See: Luke 24:38, 39; John 20:27;
1 Corinthians 15:12-19

- Deny the Trinity of God

This is the belief that God is one, singular being. They deny the existence of the Holy Spirit and Jesus as parts of the Godhead. They acknowledge Jesus Christ but not as being God.

See: Matthew 3:16, 17; John 10:30; John 14:9;
1 John 5:7

- Deny the literal second coming of Christ

This is the denial that Jesus will come again to rapture the saved and then return to reign for one thousand years before destroying the earth. This denial is because Jehovah's Witnesses teach that Jehovah will come and set them up as the rulers of the earth for eternity.

See: Acts 1:9-11; 1 Thessalonians 4:15-18; Revelation 1:7

- Salvation through works

This is the belief that you participate in your salvation by performing acts of "righteousness." Jehovah's Witnesses are some of the most dedicated door-to-door witnesses of their faith in the world. This dedication stems from their belief that they must prove themselves worthy of the Kingdom through acts of righteousness in order to be accepted by Jehovah.

See: Ephesians 2:8, 9; Titus 3:5; 1 Peter 1:17-19

Judaism

- Jews do not accept the doctrine of the Trinity

Christians worship only one God........ 1 Tim. 2:5
Let us make humankind
in our image..Gen. 1:26
The Lord Almighty ... apart from me
there is no God ....Isa. 44:6
Trinity found in Old Testament.............Isa. 48:16

- Deny that Jesus was God's son

You are my Son .... Ps. 2:7
What is His Son's Name .... Prov. 30:4
Child Born, Son is given .... Isa. 9:6

- Messiah is not to be God

Unto us a child is born … Mighty God ...... Isa. 9:6
Lord our Righteousness .... Jer. 23:5
Coming forth … from ancient days .... Mic. 5:2

- Deny the virgin birth of Jesus

God made Adam from dust
of the earth .... Gen. 2:7
Virgin birth was promised .... Isa. 7:14
Virgin born Messiah to fulfill
promise of .... Gen. 3:15

- Man does not inherit a sin nature

All follow fallen Adam .... Gen. 6:5
Heart of man corrupt .... Jer. 17:9
All stray willfully .... Isa. 53:6

- Sanctification comes thru obedience
  to the law

Abraham justified by believing .... Gen. 15:6
Believers are blessed .... Ps. 2:11, 12

- Jesus is not the Jewish Messiah

Compare Gospel accounts with Isa. 53:1-12.
Seek the Lord while he may be found;
Call upon him while he is near;
Let the wicked forsake his way,
And the unrighteous man his thoughts;

Let him return to the Lord,
That he may have compassion on him, And
to our God, for he will abundantly
pardon.. Isa. 55:6, 7

Mormon

- Man can become a god (demigod)

This is the belief that man is the offspring of
God and his wives. Therefore, as the literal
children of God, man can attain godhood of his
own planet in eternity, and he will then populate
his planet through his many wives and start his
own eternal process.

See: Psalm 51:5; Isaiah 14:12-15; Romans 3:23

- Deny the deity of Christ

Denial of Biblical fact that Jesus is God the Son
is the greatest heresy possible.

See: Matthew 1:23; John 1:1-4, 14; John 20:28;
Philippians 2:10, 11; 2 John 1:9

- Deny the resurrection of Christ

Denial of Biblical fact the literal bodily
resurrection of Jesus Christ is heresy. Many
Mormons will spiritualize the resurrection or
claim it to be figurative.

See: Luke 24:38, 39; John 20:27;
1 Corinthians 15:12-19

- Deny the Trinity of God

This is the belief that God is one, singular being.
They deny the existence of the Holy Spirit and
Jesus as parts of the Godhead.

See: Matthew 3:16, 17; John 10:30; John 14:9; 1 John 5:7

- Salvation through works

This is the belief that your salvation is predicated on performing acts of "righteousness." Mormon missionaries gather converts and names to earn their salvation and their own planet in the universe.

See: Ephesians 2:8, 9; Titus 3:5; 1 Peter 1:17-19

Reformed Theology (Calvinist)

- Total depravity of man

This is the belief that because man is so totally depraved, he has no ability to cry out to God for salvation. The only way to be saved is for God to choose you.

See: John 1:12; John 3:16; Acts 17:30, 31; 2 Peter 3:9

- Unconditional election

This is the belief that God has "sovereignly" chosen in eternity past who will and who will not go to Heaven. It is unconditional, and that includes coming to Him by faith in the blood of Christ. If He didn't choose you, you are going to Hell.

See: Romans 8:29; 1 Peter 1:1, 2

- Limited atonement

This is the belief that the atonement of Christ

is limited to those selected by God to go to Heaven. It is not a free gift offered to all who will believe, only to the chosen.

See: John 1:12; Romans 5:8; 1 Timothy 2:6

- Irresistible grace

This is the belief that God imposes His grace forcefully upon the depraved sinner and then lets him know that he is one of the "elect." You cannot resist His grace. You will be saved if God chose you, and you have neither a choice nor opinion in the matter.

See: Romans 10:9-13; James 4:7; Revelation 22:17

- Perseverance of the saints

This is the belief that only those who keep living a good life are truly the elect. Therefore, the only way to be elect is to "work out your own salvation with fear and trembling."

See: John 10:28-30; Ephesians 1:13, 14; Hebrews 13:5

Seventh Day Adventist

- Sabbath day observance

This is the belief that observing the Sabbath day is the most important law. To not keep the Sabbath is to deny the right to salvation that comes from Jehovah. Something to observe is that Jesus substituted the Sabbath day command with "Thou shalt love the Lord thy God ... ."

See: Matthew 22:36-38; Colossians 2:16, 17; Acts 20:7; 1 Corinthians 16:2

- Total annihilation

This is the belief that a denier of the "faith" will be completely annihilated. They do not believe in everlasting punishment, only in everlasting reward.

See: Mark 9:44-48; Revelation 14:10, 11; Revelation 20:10

- Deny a literal burning Hell

This is the belief that Hell is figurative, not an actual, literal place of fire.

See: Matt. 10:28; Luke 16:22, 23; Revelation 20:12-15; Revelation 21:8

- Investigative judgment

This is the belief that Christ entered the Holy of Holies in 1844 and began to investigate the actions of man to see if he is keeping the law. However, the Bible tells of only two judgments that will take place after one is dead, the Judgment seat of Christ (for the saved) and the Great White Throne (for the lost).

See: 2 Corinthians 5:9, 10; 2 Timothy 4:8; Revelation 20:11-15

- Salvation through works

This is the belief that you participate in your salvation by performing acts of "righteousness." Seventh Day Adventists believe in keeping the Old Testament laws, including the dietary laws.

See: Romans 3:19, 20, 28; Ephesians 2:8, 9;
Titus 3:5; 1 Peter 1:17-19

A Sampling of Eastern Religions
Buddhism

- The main beliefs of Buddhism

Three Universal Truths

1. Everything in life is impermanent and constantly changing.
2. Because nothing is permanent, a life based on possessions or relationships does not make you happy.
3. There is no eternal, unchanging soul and "self" is just a collection of changing characteristics or attributes.

- The Four Noble Truths are the essence of Buddhism

1. Life consists of suffering. This suffering taints every aspect of life.
2. Suffering has a cause, which is craving and attachment.
3. Suffering can end, and nirvana can be obtained.
4. The Noble Eightfold Path leads to the end of all our worldly suffering.

- The Noble Eightfold Path

Buddha taught people not to worship him as a god. He said they should take responsibility for their own lives and actions. Buddha also taught that the "middle" between self-indulgence and self-denial is the path to happiness. The "middle" or Eightfold Path is the path to enlightenment or nirvana (a state in which any living thing is free from pain and sorrow). By living a life with compassion and love for all, we achieve liberation from selfish desires and a peace that is ultimately more fulfilling than anything we experience by indulging in pleasure. The "middle" or Eightfold Path brings deliverance from Samsara, the painful cycle of rebirth and reincarnation. Death is a constant cycle of reincarnation until we achieve enlightenment.

- The Eightfold Path entails 8 practices

1. Right view: A correct understanding of the Four Noble Truths and the nature of things
2. Right intention: Avoid thoughts of attachment, hate and harm
3. Right speech: Don't lie or speak harshly; don't indulge in divisive speech
4. Right action: Avoid killing, stealing and sexual overindulgence
5. Right livelihood: Steer clear of anything that can directly or indirectly harm others, such as the slave trade, the sale of weapons, drugs and alcohol, poison or animal slaughter
6. Right effort: Maintain a positive state of mind and let go of negativity
7. Right mindfulness: Be aware of your body, feelings and thoughts

8. Right concentration: Meditation which leads to detachment and the removal of negativity from one's thought processes

- The Five Precepts (Codes of Conduct)

The underlying principle of the Five Precepts in Buddhism is the avoidance of abuse to yourself or others. These precepts are the foundation of all Buddhist philosophies. Once you have developed your ethical base, much stress and emotional conflict can be avoided, allowing for conscious choices and commitment to your path.

Focus is on free choice and intention. There are no commandments in Buddhism, only choices that build karma. Each precept is a vow or promise to oneself.

- Buddhists abstain from:

1. Killing of any living being
2. Stealing
3. Sexual misconduct
4. Lying or false speech
5. Intoxication (alcohol and drugs)

- Karma

Karma in Buddhism is explained as action driven by intention. These actions lead to consequences (cause and effect). When we mindlessly follow our actions, we are led to rebirth or reincarnation (samsara). But the Noble Eightfold Path leads to nirvana and shows us how to end samsara and attain enlightenment.

- Tripitaka

After Buddha died, his teachings were casually written down from what people remembered. The Tripitaka, or The Three Baskets, is a collection of Buddha's teachings and sermons.

- Buddhism is more a way of life than a religion.

Hinduism

Hinduism does not have an official set of beliefs; consequently, there is no formal creed one must accept to be Hindu. Instead, Hinduism is a most diverse set of religious beliefs and practices. Nevertheless, in an attempt to make sense of the broadness of Hinduism, the following is a list of some common beliefs that Hindus accept as part of their tradition:

- Brahman: There is one supreme, impersonal reality called Brahman. Brahman is the source of all things but is not a personal creator. Brahman is, rather, the divine essence of all that exists. Brahman is impersonal, eternal and beyond all human comprehension.

- The Atman/Brahman Unity: Most adherents of Hinduism believe that, in their true selves (atman), they are an extension from and one with Brahman. Our essence is identical to that of Brahman.

- Individual souls are immortal: A Hindu believes that the individual soul is neither created nor destroyed; it has been, it is, and it will be. Actions of the soul while residing in a body require that it reap the consequences of those actions in the next life — the same soul in a different body. The process of movement of the atman from one body to another is known as reincarnation or transmigration. The kind of body the soul inhabits next is determined by karma (actions accumulated in previous lives).

- Cyclical View of Time: Hindus do not understand time as a progression from a definite past toward a distinct future. Instead, Hindus see reality as a recurring cycle that happens again and again. Hindus believe that the universe undergoes endless cycles of creation, preservation and dissolution. Brahman is the manifestation of the universe, then returns to a perfect unity, then manifests as the universe again. This view of time is one of the significant differences between Hinduism and Western modes of thinking. We view time as linear, while the Hindus view time as cyclical.

- Karma: According to Hinduism, our primary problem is ignorance of our divine nature. We have forgotten that we are extensions of Brahman and attached ourselves to the desires of our separate selves or egos. The law of karma is essentially the moral equivalent of a natural law of cause and effect. It basically says that we reap what we sow. However, our actions affect us not only in the present life but on into future lives, which is why reincarnation exists. Any act of personal will is karma, and its effects keep us bound in the endless cycle of reincarnation. So long as we act on personal desires, good or bad, we remain in the suffering of samsara.

- Samsara: Samsara is the perpetual cycle of birth, death, and rebirth that an individual endures until the balance of their karma is removed. Rebirth is not desirable in Hinduism, and the cycle perpetuates all suffering. Any deliberate action of the will, whether good or bad, is Karma and will lead to a future life. The ultimate goal is not to have "good karma" rather than "bad karma." Instead, it is to have no karma at all and thus to escape samsara entirely. To accomplish this, one must live without acting on personal desire or ambition. Disconnected from desire and free from remaining karma, one can transcend samsara into moksha.

- Moksha: The goal of the individual soul is moksha. This liberation of the soul from samsara enables the attaining of true enlightenment. It means the realization of one's union with the universal essence of Brahman, and thus one's complete union with all things. Atman is one with Brahman, and the individual is no longer reborn in the world of distinct objects and beings.

- Gods and Goddesses: Many Hindus worship various gods and goddesses. They often believe these beings can be appeased or appealed to through rituals and offerings in a temple, at a home shrine, by a sacred river or in other places. Consequently, they worship millions of local and household gods.

- Enlightened Masters: Many Hindus accept various enlightened masters, avatars or people who can serve as guides to faithful Hindus. These individuals serve as examples and provide direction for those who want to achieve moksha or enlightenment from the suffering of samsara.

- Ahimsa: Ahimsa means nonviolence to life. Hindus have great respect for all life-forms and seek to cause the least amount of harm possible. This respect for life applies not just to humans but also to animals.

- Scripture: Hindus believe the four Vedas are holy and sacred texts, but this does not mean that a Hindu must regard them as literally true or practice everything taught within them. "Truth" is eternal.

- No One True Religion: Hindus believe there are many paths to Brahman. There is no one true religion or one right way to find Brahman.

- The Caste System: Historically, Hindu societies have operated within a strict form of caste system in which one was born into a specific class that would determine one's career and place in society. The Caste System has since been legally disbanded in India. Nevertheless, many of the ideas of the Caste System are socially ingrained and have proven difficult to remove.

Islam

Islam teaches on a multitude of topics. It is monotheistic, denies the deity of Christ, the Trinity and salvation by grace alone. Salvation in Islam is by sincere repentance with the hope that Allah will forgive the Muslim. However, Islam teaches the only way to be sure to go to Heaven is to die in holy war or Jihad. All references are to the Quran (Koran).

- Doctrines of Islam on God

1. There is only one God (5:73; 112:1-4).
2. God is called Allah by Muslims (5:73).
3. Allah sees all things (40:20) and is present everywhere (2:115; 7:7).

4. Allah is the sole creator and sustainer of the universe (3:191).
5. Allah is not a Trinity but is one (5:73).
6. Allah is all-knowing (2:268; 10:61) and all-powerful (6:61, 62).
7. Allah created Heaven and earth (2:29; 6:1, 73; 25:61, 62; 36:81; 46:33).

- Salvation and Judgment

1. Allah will judge all people on the day of judgment (3:30; 35:33-37; 99:6-8).
2. If your good deeds exceed your bad deeds and you believe in Allah and sincerely repent of sins, you may go to Heaven (3:135; 7:8, 9; 21:47; 49:14; 66:8, 9).
3. There is an eternal Hell for those who are not Muslims, not practicing Islam and not of the true faith (3:77).
4. Hell is a place of unlimited capacity (50:30), eternal torment (2:39; 14:17; 25:65; 39:26), fire (9:63; 11:16; 25:11, 12; 104:6, 7), with boiling water (38:55-58; 55:43, 44), where skin is burned and renewed (4:56), for unbelievers (3:13; 19:49) and Jinn (11:119) with faces covered with fire (14:49, 50).
5. There is a tree in Hell, named Tree of Zaqqum, from which bad fruit is produced and the damned are forced to eat (37:62-67; 44:43-48; 56:52-55).
6. Heaven (Paradise), a Garden (79:41) of bliss and fruit (69:21-24), has rivers (3:198),

with maidens pure and holy (4:57), and carpets and cushions (88:8-16).

7. There will be a physical resurrection of all people (19:93-95) on the Day of Judgment (3:77; 15:25; 16:38; 42:29).

8. Judgment is based on a person's sincere repentance (66:8, 9) and righteous deeds (5:9; 24:26; 45:21; 22; 64:7).

- Other Doctrines of Islam

1. There is an after-life (2:154; 75:12).

2. There are such things as angels, created by Allah, made from light. Angels are obedient slaves incapable of refusing to do Allah's will.

3. The angel Gabriel brought the revelation of the Koran to Muhammad (2:97; 16:102).

4. There is no actual verse where the Holy Spirit is said to be Gabriel or identified as Gabriel. These verses show that both the Holy Spirit and Gabriel brought down the revelation.

5. Jinn are unseen beings, created (51:56) from fire (15:27; 55:15) but are not angels. They have communities. There are good and bad Jinn.

6. The Devil, called Iblis (2:34), is an evil Jinn.

7. Jesus was a great prophet but not the Son of God (9:30), is not divine (5:17, 75) and was not crucified (4:157).

8. Muhammad is Allah's greatest and last prophet, and his message supersedes all other past prophets, including Jesus.

9. The Koran is Allah's word, and he literally spoke it to Gabriel, who gave it to Muhammad.

10. There are other holy writings, such as the Torah, the first five books of Moses and the Psalms, but the Koran supersedes them all.

11. Pre-ordainment (Qadar) is the teaching that all things, good and bad, are preordained to occur.

12. Fasting is to be observed during the month of Ramadan (2:185).

13. Drinking alcohol is forbidden (2:219; 4;43; 5:93, 94; 16:67).

14. Gambling is forbidden (2:219; 5:90-94).

15. Man is made from the dust of the earth (23:12).

16. There is no last-minute repentance (4:18).

DIFFERENT TYPES OF PEOPLE WE WILL ENCOUNTER

Let's look at some different types of people we will encounter when we evangelize. By looking at the Scriptures, we can find parallel stories to relate to each type of individual. Sometimes when we present passages the lost can connect with, they become more receptive to the Give 'em Jesus Scriptures.

1. The religious person who is set in their ways and thinks they already know everything — An excellent place to start is the story of Nicodemus found in John 3:1-10. Nicodemus had excellent qualities: a teacher of the law, a member of the Pharisees and very well educated. He was torn between Jesus and His words, and retaining his status as a Jewish religious leader. Jesus told him he must be born again by the Spirit of God. **Every believer must be born again!**

2. The hurt or wounded person — This individual needs words of comfort and hope. You can use the story of the Good Samaritan in Luke 10:30-35. Jesus is the Good Samaritan and He loves regardless of the situation. He can bring peace, forgiveness and comfort to the soul like no one else.

3. The hopeless person — This may be someone who has only a few hours to live. You might use the story of the thief on the cross. His situation certainly looked hopeless. Use Luke 23:39-43. The thief realized his end had come and confessed his sins to Jesus. Then he called on Jesus to remember him when He came into His glory. Jesus responded, "Today, you will be with Me in paradise."

4. The person heavily burdened with guilt — This individual is living in defeat under a burden of condemnation and sin consciousness. The story of the Prodigal son in Luke 15:11-23 might best fit this person. This son lived a lifestyle of selfish desire, which led to a life of destruction. After he hit life's bottom, he looked up and repented. He desired to be delivered by returning to his father's house. There he found love, forgiveness, acceptance and a reinstatement of his sonship.

5. The doubter who believes only what he can see — Use the story about Thomas, one of Jesus' disciples in John 20:24-29. He believed only what he saw because he had a "doubting" faith. After the resurrection, Jesus personally visited him and revealed Himself in His resurrected body to Thomas. Thomas, then, believed and confessed

Him as God. True faith is that of Abraham who took God at His word by faith, and God made of Him a great nation.

6. The church-rejected person — The story of the adulteress woman found in John 8:1-11 is a good evangelizing tool for this person. She was accused of adultery by the religious leaders and, thus, condemned by the law. But, Jesus came to her aid. Even when the synagogue leaders rejected her, Jesus came to her defense with a loving act of forgiveness. The accusers all left, and Jesus restored her. He said, "Neither do I condemn you. Go and sin no more!" We must encourage them to seek restoration back into the fellowship of the church.

7. Spiritually lost and physically sick — The story of the ill slave who worked for the Roman centurion in Matthew 8:5-13 is an excellent place to start for this person. Faith in God has a powerful effect no matter the distance we proclaim God's Word and invoke His healing power. Faith carries power to change things in the natural world. Jesus is always willing and able to heal. So, if a person will ask in faith, believing they receive, they can be saved and, sometimes, healed simultaneously.

8. The bereaved individual struggling from the loss of a loved one — This is an

excellent time to share the Gospel. They can find hope in I Thessalonians 4:13-18, where we see a reunion of believers with their loved ones at the rapture of the Church. This promise of reunion can certainly be a comfort for believers.

9. The person living in rebellion against God, the Word of God, the Church and other believers — They love to call the church and God's people "hypocrites." Unfortunately, these accusations can sometimes be true. A practical place to take this person is to the story of Saul, whom God renamed Paul after his conversion on the road to Damascus, found in Acts 9:1-6. Paul had search warrants to apprehend the people of God and may have even been a serial killer. But, when Paul came face-to-face with the risen Jesus, he repented and became a follower who later wrote over half of our New Testament. When he surrendered his heart to Jesus, he gave the rest of his life to the service of God. There has never been a sinner that God cannot change! Many times those who experience radical transformations become God's most faithful servants.

10. The backslider — If you are not moving forward in your spiritual walk, you are automatically regressing. The night before

Jesus was crucified, Peter assured Jesus that he would never turn his back on Him. However, his inability to recognize his own weakness, neglect of prayer and distancing himself from Jesus resulted in his denial of Jesus. Too much of the world to be happy in the Lord and too much of the Lord to be happy in the world creates a most miserable person. But, only days later, Jesus reassured Peter of His love and trust. Failure is not final with God! (Luke 22:31-34, 39-45, 54-62, John 21:15-17)

11. The atheist — This person generally has no genuine concept of God and His power to transform. You may want to use the story of Simon, the sorcerer who exploited witchcraft to generate wealth. In Acts 8:4-25, Phillip was sent by God to preach the message of the cross to Samaria. Along with his message, revival came to Samaria, and many were saved and healed. God then sent Peter and John from Jerusalem with the power of the Holy Spirit. When Simon saw the magnitude of this power from God, he was so overwhelmed that he offered money to buy this Holy Spirit power from Peter. Peter responded, "Repent of your wickedness and pray that God would forgive you!" Simon asked Peter to pray to God for his deliverance from sin and error. God can transform any sinner!

12. The independent materialist — This person trusts in wealth for future security. He typically likes wealth that he can see and touch. Matthew 6:19-24 would be an excellent place to go for this person. Jesus warns against laying up treasures on earth instead of in Heaven. Our hearts will always be where our treasure is. Earthly treasures rust, rot or get eaten by moths. When we store up heavenly treasures, our hearts will stay focused on the eternal things that will last forever. (1 John 2:16, 17; 1 Timothy 6:9, 10)

13. Those suffering from peer pressure, bullying, human trafficking and other forms of oppression — Many in our society of all ages suffer from depression. We live in an era of instantaneous communication, yet, many feel lonely, left out and left behind. Our culture is judgmental and seems to garner much satisfaction from watching others suffer in pain. Here are a few passages that we could apply:

    Romans 8:33-39
    Romans 12:14-21
    Psalms 10:17
    Psalms 37:9
    Psalms 103:6
    Psalms 140:12

Sometimes the best way to the Gospel is through people's problems. When we can identify categorically with those to whom we are witnessing, this tool can sometimes be a gentle way to transition to the Give 'em Jesus Scriptures. The Scriptures are our ultimate destination. The salvation Scriptures are where we get to watch the Holy Spirit move!

CHAPTER 6

CHAPTER 7

A FEW PARTING THOUGHTS

In the hundreds of churches I have had the privilege to speak in over the last 20 years, a common theme that resonates is, "We want revival!" The people of God want to see revival in our Church. We envision a restoration of the Church back to a first-century evangelism machine with Pentecostal growth found in the book of Acts. We want to see a reawakening in the hearts of individuals, families, communities and our nation. But in reality, while we talk about and wait on God to pour out His sovereign Spirit on the Church, we, as God's people, sit mired in our comfort zones.

It certainly appears as though we do not believe in evangelism anymore. Are we so oblivious that we have convinced ourselves the spiritually lost no longer exist or are unimportant? I don't think so. Or, do we perceive it politically incorrect to search out the lost? Or, have we, maybe even subconsciously, chosen to outsource our evangelism responsibility? But, to whom? History has proven that revival never comes unless we, as God's people, sow the seeds of the Good News of Jesus Christ.

According to the Baptist News Global, in an article dated May 28, 2019, the last pre-pandemic year, the Southern Baptist Church reported the lowest number of believer baptisms since WWII. That represents a decrease of 55% from a peak in 1972. Yet, the number of Southern Baptist Churches is up 113%. If believer's baptism, one of the most fundamental doctrines of evangelical Christianity, is a measurement for reaching the lost, the body of Christ is in serious need of a tune-up. Sadly, reaching the spiritually lost has proven to be an immensely challenging mission for all mainline protestant denominations in America!

One particular denomination conducted a survey of its leadership. Two statistics that stand out are:

- 99% believe that every Christian is under command to preach the Gospel to a lost world.
- 96% believe their churches would have grown more if they had been more involved in evangelism.

But what is most perplexing, among all evangelicals today, less than 2% are involved in the ministry of evangelism, clearly explaining why 95% have never led one other person to Jesus. Perhaps, complacency has quenched our passion for the lost, and reaching the lost is, without doubt, no longer a high priority. Why are we stuck in neutral? Irrespective of the reason, we are not experiencing the joy that sharing our faith generates! Philemon 6 says, "and I pray that the sharing of your faith may become effective for the full knowledge of every good thing that is in us for the sake of Christ."

Conversely, we have settled for the sin of deathlike silence while God is looking for industrial strength "fishers of men" to reclaim our country and our world for Christ! The associated disease is spiritual dryness and lukewarmness. And, here we sit, with a debilitating misfire in our spiritual engine.

God wants to use us! Yet, we defer getting prepared into the future and fail to experience those precious moments God has prepared for us. And, they become yet another "If only ..." moment! When God opens the door, are we going to be ready? Where ever God is calling you, the Holy Spirit is already working. Where God guides, God provides. We must seize the moment. **Now!** Time is critical!

Remember, success is not leading someone to Christ. Success is sharing your faith, living your life out for Jesus, and sowing the seed of the Good News. God doesn't call us to be successful. He calls us to be obedient.

Personal witnessing is not just about the spiritually lost. After all, if we refuse, God can "make the rocks cry out"! It is about experiencing God in all His fullness, healing spiritual dryness, and experiencing a new walk with Jesus that will transform your life with a new spirit of excitement. God wants us to experience His joy!

We almost always find two commonalities where we find Jesus engaged in evangelism. Whether it's Nicodemus, the Samaritan woman at the well, the rich young ruler, the lawyer or others, we see Jesus engaged in one-on-one, conversational evangelism. Jesus sought out the lost with His personal signature style of communication. 87% of new believers come to Christ through this Jesus-style evangelism. I want to be like Jesus!

Choose the verses for your application that you find most compelling: Romans, the Gospel of John, Isaiah, etc. Memorize those verses. Underline or highlight those verses and write the next verse beside the current verse for quick and smooth progression. I prefer to use small Testaments with my verses of choice already neatly composed inside the back cover. Or, you can use this Handbook. Always be familiar with your Scripture source. Use what works best for your application. Stay focused on the Scriptures. They are "the power of God." (Romans 1:16)

Always wear a smile and speak the truth with love. No one has ever been argued or coerced into the Kingdom of Heaven. Any person you can argue into the Kingdom of Heaven, Satan will argue out faster. No one ever received Jesus because he prayed a prayer just to get rid of an annoying soul winner! Do not force yourself or the Gospel on anyone. Always be perceptive and search for that person who wants to hear the message of the cross. As you apply the simple steps laid out in this book, you will witness many decisions for Christ!

Satan's second biggest lie ever propagated on humanity is, "Your witness for Jesus is not important." I don't know what to say, so I'll let someone else do it. I will be ridiculed and rejected, so I'll let someone else do it. But, regardless of your excuse, our witness for Jesus is critically essential to the work of the Kingdom. What I have learned is this: most assuredly, someone else can always do it better than me or, perhaps, you. However, nobody can do God's will for my life but me. Nobody can do God's will for your life but you. The heart of the matter is this, when we are prepared, even on our worst day, we are good enough for God! And, **He will use even us!**

I pray that God will use this Handbook as a catalyst for awareness and preparedness to execute passionate evangelism! It will guide you as you mold your skill set around your personality type. Once you build your skill set, you will develop a sense of comfort and confidence. You will see it bear fruit continuously, at which point your focus will shift. Your skill set will then morph into a mindset as you focus on God's next open door. Then, we become soul-winning intentional. This Handbook will bring you into compliance with Jesus' command to be "fishers of men"!

It's time to go to work!!

CHAPTER 7

APPENDIX 1

4 Easy Steps for Sharing the Gospel in 4 Minutes

Step 1: The Engagement Questions

1. Did you know there is a God in Heaven who loves you?
2. Is there something in your life that I can pray for?
3. Have you ever considered becoming a Christian?
4. Where do you go to church?
5. Do you have a church that you call home?
6. Does this world ever make you feel insecure?
7. Has anyone ever explained to you the difference between religion and a relationship with Jesus Christ?
8. Has anyone ever explained Christianity to you?
9. I experience some of those same problems in my life as well. By the way, I've found a solution for my pain. May I share that with you?
10. Do you have a copy of the New Testament?
11. This world seems to be on a collision course with disaster. If that disaster occurred today, have you ever wondered where you would take your next breath?
12. May I give you a one-minute spiritual survey that can change your life?

13. You know about my spiritual beliefs, but I don't know about yours. What are they?
14. Do you consider salvation something that you are working toward?
15. If you were standing before God right now and He were to ask you, "Why should I let you into My Heaven?" how would you respond?
16. Would you like to receive God's free gift of eternal life today?
17. May I have permission to share five Scriptures that changed my life?
18. Does truth matter to you?
19. May I share with you how a relationship with Jesus Christ changed my life?
20. Do you ever ask yourself: Who am I? Where am I going? What will happen to me when I die?

(You may add others that give you a comfort level in transitioning to the Spiritual Thermometer.)

Step 2:
The Spiritual Thermometer Questions

1. Do you have any spiritual beliefs?
2. Do you believe in Jesus? Who do you think he was?
3. Do you believe there is a Heaven and a Hell?
4. If you died today, where would you go? If Heaven, why?
5. If we could wind the clock of your life backward, would there be a time where we found you on your knees inviting Jesus into your heart?
6. By the way, if what you believe is not true, would you want to know?

The "Acid" Question

"May I ask you, what for me, is the most important question in the world? On a scale of 0%-100%, how certain are you that if you die today, you would spend eternity in Heaven?"

After applying the Spiritual Thermometer, if they test Holy Spirit positive and meter at anything less than 100%, you should ask, "May I share some Scripture with you that I believe might give you insight on this matter?" If the answer is "Yes," move to the Give 'em Jesus Scriptures. Move as promptly to the Scriptures as possible. If the answer is "No," try to get the Testament in their hands with a commitment to read the back two pages today! **The Scriptures**

**are where the power is! However, no matter
what happens at this point, you have been
successful. You have been obedient to share
the Gospel, and the results belong to God!
God will honor his Word.**

Step 3:
The Give 'em Jesus Scriptures

1. John 3:16 — God's Love

*"For God so loved the world, that he gave
his only Son, that whoever believes in him
should not perish but have eternal life."*

2. Romans 3:23 — Man's Sin

*"For all have sinned and fall short of the
glory of God."*

3. Romans 6:23 — God's Remedy

*"For the wages of sin is death, but the free gift
of God is eternal life in Christ Jesus our Lord."*

4. Revelation 3:20 — God's Call

*"Behold I stand at the door and knock. If
anyone hears my voice and opens the door,
I will come in to him."*

5. John 1:12 — Man's Choice

*"But to all who did receive him, who believed
in his name, he gave the right to become
children of God."*

Step 4:
The Gospel Review Questions

1. "Do you understand that God loves you?"

2. "Do you understand that you are a sinner in need of forgiveness?"

3. "Do you understand that Jesus died for full payment of your sins so you will have eternal life in Heaven?"

4. "Do you understand that God is knocking at the door of your heart?"

5. "God promises salvation and eternal life in Heaven to every person who professes faith in Jesus, 100% guaranteed. Are you ready to invite Jesus into your heart?"

(If you prefer, you can use the 5 Gospel Review Questions that I laid out in The 5 Undeniable Truths Approach beginning on page 29.)

The Sinner's Prayer

God, from my heart, I admit to You that I am a sinner and I ask for Your forgiveness. I believe that Your Son, Jesus, took the punishment I deserve by shedding His blood on the cross. He gave His life as the full payment for my sins and rose again from the dead. Thank you for changing my heart. I now confess and turn from my sins and receive Your Son, Jesus, as my Savior and Lord. Amen

The Great Confession

I believe that Jesus is the Christ, the Son of the living God. Who died for my sins: past, present and future — 100% of the time. And I confess Him as my personal Lord and Savior.

The "Why?" Principle

You: "Are you ready to invite Jesus Christ into your life?"

Friend: "No."

You: "Why?"

Friend: "I'm not ready."

You: "Why?"

Remember — This is not a debate, an argument, a tug-of-war, etc. Do this with "meekness and gentleness"! (1 Peter 3:15)

New Believer Questions

1. How many of your sins did Jesus die for?

2. On Judgment Day, will you be innocent or guilty?

3. Do you know where Jesus is living today?

4. Who has been praying for you?

5. Do you know where your friend goes to church?

6. Do you know your friend's phone number? Let's call that person now!

7. May I take you to church with me?

8. Read the book of 1John today.

9. I will call you tomorrow to see if the Word became different.

APPENDIX 2

OVERCOMING OBJECTIONS

APPENDIX 3

A Biographical Sketch

It was October 1974 in room 309-C Kitchen House dorm, Wake Forest University when I heard the knock on my door. The two young men were from Piedmont Bible College. They were concerned about one thing, the salvation of my soul! I was "born again" at age 12. I attended church regularly. But, at this point, I was 19 years old and could not articulate my faith. I failed their test! This incident left me feeling guilty and empty but not bad enough that I wanted to do something about my inability!

In Dececmber 1986 at age 32, I became one of the youngest franchise automobile dealers in the country. By 1988, I was the largest volume Chrysler-Jeep dealer in the two Carolinas with a dream of acquiring more franchises and locations. But, by 1994, the "pursuit of worldly gain" had left me spiritually depleted. I had banished God to the back seat of my life. Now, it was time to put Him back in the driver's seat where He belonged. With vehicle production and sales at the highest level in our nation's history, I sold my franchise and walked away.

I could never forget that night in 309-C. Since then, God had put multitudes of people in my path for the express purpose of sharing the life changing message of the cross. I let God down,

time after time. But, as an accumulating effect
of all those years, I could not stand the guilt one
more day. I enrolled in Piedmont Bible College
(now Piedmont International University) to
study Personal Witnessing and Evangelism. In
the early days, I was so scared that when I had
to share my faith to meet class requirements, I
hid in the smoking section of an old mall where
I was sure I would not see anyone I knew.

A young alumnus, David Tinsley, a missionary
to New York City, taught the "on-the-job"
portion of the class. One afternoon in the area
of 28th St. and Cleveland Ave. in Winston-
Salem, NC, I hid in the proverbial bushes and
watched David lead a young lady with acute
Sickle Cell Disease to Jesus while sitting on
the front bumper of his old specially prepared
missionary van. While watching her tears
puddle on that asphalt parking lot, the spiritual
power of that moment changed both of us
forever. The spiritual power blew me away!
I wanted to experience that power, just one
more time, more than anything in the world.

A few weeks later, I was on the Central Piedmont
Community College campus in Charlotte, NC. I
engaged a young Asian lady with my Testament.
She told me she was Hindu and, consequently,
could not touch the Testament. I prayed for
10 seconds (she was late for class) and offered
her the Testament a second time. Ever so

cautiously, she accepted it. I asked her to start reading on page 450 (the book of 1 John). As she walked away, I heard her mumble, "Page 450."

About 3 hours later that afternoon, at a different location on campus, she approached me holding her Testament. I asked, "Are you ready to receive Jesus into your heart?" She said, "Yes!" Along with her, she brought two other students. One was a young man with special needs, and both prayed to receive Jesus into their hearts, too!

After about 2 months, of applying the simple soul-winning steps outlined in Chapter 2 of this Handbook, I witnessed over 65 people make decisions for Jesus. At this point, God convicted me that measuring the harvest is not my job. He "keeps the books"! He is Lord of the harvest — always! My job is to sow seed. My responsibility is always to be prepared and continuously refine my skill set.

Having shared my faith through one-on-one evangelism with, if I had to guess, over 5,000 people during the last 20 years, God has put a new calling on my life. That calling is to help the body of Christ around the world prepare themselves to be practical, passionate soul winners. That is what this book is all about. We are wasting precious time! Jesus said, **"It's time to go!"**

ENDNOTES

Chapter 4

Soul Winner's Guide by Max E. Zimmermann (published by Immanuel Mission, Inc. Phoenix, AZ). Copyright 1948, renewed 1976 and is no longer in print. Mr. Zimmermann compiled some of the objections, Scripture phrases and verse references. Scripture in Chapter 4 is quoted from The Holy Bible, King James Version.

Chapter 5

Some of the Eastern religions information was provided by CARM.org. —The Christian Apologetics Research Ministry.

All Scriptures in this book, unless otherwise noted, are quoted from The Holy Bible, ESV (English Standard Version). Copyright, 2001 by Crossway, a publishing ministry of Good News Publishers.

All statistics in this book, unless otherwise noted, are from Bible.org.

SPECIAL ACKNOWLEDGEMENTS

To mother and dad, you etched Jesus on my heart. Dad, you were a rock-solid man of God in our home and to our family. If I could clone you, I could change the world!

To my wife Rene, for the countless times you proofed my scripts and for your patient enduring of all the hours.

To Bill Fay and Linda Shepherd — Share Jesus Without Fear. It is the most powerful personal witnessing book on the face of the earth. Bill, your training was priceless! I will forever wear your influence on my life. I am eternally grateful!

To The Gideon Ministry, for all of the open doors that you afford, for the best quality Testaments and resources but, most importantly, for all of the memories!

To Michael Griffith, you are always ready to go with me wherever God opens a door. Thanks for your faithfulness to the work of the Kingdom!

To the leadership of Grandview Pines Baptist Church there in Millbrook, Al., thanks for your contribution. To God be the glory!

To you guys from Piedmont Bible College who knocked on the door of Suite 309 Kitchen House Dorm. Thanks! You were an inspiration!

To David Tinsley, thanks for the vision that I caught there on 28th St. and Cleveland Ave. in Winston-Salem, NC. The roots of this book germinated there.

To Dana at dclinedesign. You can "part the Red Sea" with that computer. Thanks for your patience and expertise!

To Georgia Akers. If not for you, I would never have survived the "fiery furnace"!

To all who read this book and honor God's call to be "fishers of men,"

Give 'em JESUS!!

Kevin C.   Nutrition Center Asst. Store Mgr. — Thomasville, NC

It was the worst day of my life; sitting in the county jail, wearing a suicide "Turtle Suit" and facing up to 15 years in prison. Thoughts were spinning in my head like a pinwheel when an unassuming man approached the bars and said, "Sir, may I give you this Testament?" I stepped to the bars intending to say, "No" but for some reason I said "Yes" and it changed my life right then and there.

That man's name was Fred Hege and, while he says he was just the messenger, God sends the right person for the situation. His message was of salvation and redemption. His mission is to bring the redeeming message of the cross and Jesus Christ to the lost. I served 6.5 years. He was the right messenger with the right message. I now have a personal relationship with Jesus. I am a 2 Corinthians 5:17 "New Creation" in Christ!

John 4:35
*35"... Look, I tell you, lift up your eyes, and see that **the fields are white for harvest.** 36Already the one who reaps is receiving wages and gathering fruit for eternal life, so that sower and reaper may rejoice together."*

Proverbs 11:30 (KJV)
*30The fruit of the righteous is a tree of life; and **he that winneth souls is wise.***

If sinners be damned, at least let them leap to Hell over our bodies. If they will perish, let them perish with our arms about their knees. Let no one go there unwarned and unprayed for.
—Charles H. Spurgeon

Share your experiences and testimonies with the world at justgiveemjesus.org (just give em jesus .org)